Once Upon a Rhyme

London
Edited by Claire Tupholme

First published in Great Britain in 2011 by:

Young Writers
Remus House
Coltsfoot Drive
Peterborough
PE2 9BF
Telephone: 01733 890066
Website: www.youngwriters.co.uk

All Rights Reserved
Book Design by Tim Christian
© Copyright Contributors 2011
SB ISBN 978-0-85739-489-7

THIS BOOK BELONGS TO

....

Foreword

Here at Young Writers our objective is to help children discover the joys of poetry and creative writing. Few things are more encouraging for the aspiring writer than seeing their own work in print. We are proud that our anthologies are able to give young authors this unique sense of confidence and pride in their abilities.

Once Upon A Rhyme is our latest fantastic competition, specifically designed to encourage the writing skills of primary school children through the medium of poetry. From the high quality of entries received, it is clear that Once Upon A Rhyme really captured the imagination of all involved.

The resulting collection is an excellent showcase for the poetic talents of the younger generation and we are sure you will be charmed and inspired by it, both now and in the future.

Contents

Maddie Stewart is our featured poet this year. She has written a nonsense workshop for you and included some of her great poems. You can find these at the end of your book

All Souls CE Primary School, Westminster
Shelby Tayab Dosdos (10) 1
Theo Turan (10) 2
Immanuel Ogendo (10) 2
Alison Weaver (10) 3
Cleah Black (10) 3
Sameer Wahid (10) 4
Ellie Simmons (10) 4
Eyasin Ali (10) 5
Raania Hammoudan (9) 5
Lily Pearce (11) 6
Nell Cronin (9) 6
Daniella Pollendine (10) 7
Sharika Ahmed (9) 7
Leo Blanchet (10) 8
Tife Adegbemile (10) 8
Jake Brindle (10) 9
Kira Miller (11) 9

Barclay Primary School, Leyton
Anastasia Theodorou (10) 10
Ashutosh Khatri (10) 10
Saarah Hossany (10) 11
Darren Kaj (10) 11
Wissam Nahi (10) 12

Buxton School Primary Phase, Leytonstone
Mariam Olusunmade (10) 12

Essendine Primary School, Maida Vale
Mariam Olusunmade (10) 12
Jonald Rakipaj (11) 13
Asil Ibrahim (11) 14
Rami Bettache (11) 15
Yassir Mahdi (11) 16
Dreni Muhaxheri (10) 17
Qamil Pajaziti (11) 18
Tasnima Islam (10) 19
Hanna Abdalla (11) 20
Aishah Begum (10) 21
Ali Hussain (11) 22
Imaan Magou (10) 23
Yassmine Fadley Mtiri (11) 24
Bronte Paul (10) 24
Tahani Mahamud (10) 25
Muminul Islam (10) 25
Billal Damouche (10) 26
Artin Pacolli (10) 27
Eldin Hasanovic (10) 28
Nabila Hussain (10) 29
Muhammad Abu Bakar (10) 29
Albin Salihu (11) 30
Chidima Akopoazu (10) 30

Heathfield House School, Chiswick
Sarah Delabriere (10) 31
Ella Hourican (7) 32
Evie White (11) 33

Heber Primary School, Southwark
Esther Chemla (9) 33
Ruben Bø Dower (11) 34
Isaac St Louis (8) 34
Georgia Muraszko (9) 35
Myles Williams (9) 35
Marika Ryan (10) 36
Samantha Dobson (9) 36
Isabel Nelson (10) 37
Ella Pound (10) 37
Jayden Neil-White (11) 38
Jay Hailstone Collier (10) 38
Elizabeth Linke (8) 39
Ruairidh Higgins (9) 39
Tyan Benjamin (9) 40
Victoria Adeyeye (9) 40
Ruby Redman (9) 41
Chloe Sanguyu Harris (9) 41
Louisa Underhill (9) 42

Horn Park Primary School, Lee
Louis Ashley-Brown (11) 42
Emily Ashcroft (11) 43
Philips Obakpolor (10) 44
Kasey Bullen (11) 45
Ahmet Akis (11) 46
Shauna Millard (11) 47
Loveshan Selvarajah (10) 47
Morgan Spencer (10) 48
Arry Downey (11) 48
Rebecca Cladingboel (10) 49
Caris Toomer-Willis (10) 49
Jordan Ellis-Campbell &
Rebekah Ahmed (10) 50
Adam Wiggins (11) & Ben Carberry (10) .. 50
Jedd Rawlings (11) 51
Ahmet Akis 51
Alfie Hadley (10) & Steven Hayes (11) 51

Lawdale Junior School, Bethnal Green
Mohammed Sajid Hoque (8) 52
Sumayya Hoque (10) 52
Naznina Begum (10) 53
Sabrina Akthar (9) 54
Cyma Aktar (11) 55

Moumi Qurayshi (9) 56
Masuma Rahman (11) 56
Jannah Yeasmin (11) 57
Hajara Jarrin (10) 57
Anisah Begum Ali (11) 58
Radia Aktar (10) 58
Inayah Naima (9) 59
Mohammed Rabbi (11) 59
Taklima Yesmin (9) 60
Tasnia Aktar (11) 60
Fariha Ishrat (9) 61

Redriff Primary School, Rotherhithe
Nikita Mwanza (8) 61
Archie Mehmet (9) 61
Suad Jones (8) 62
Kiara Rowe (7) 62
Gracie Hicks (7) 63
Molly Easter (8) 63
Denise Nantongo (9) 63
Aparajita Sandhu (8) 64
Lily-Rose Payne (7) 64
Finn Lawless (7) 64
Carl West (8) 65
Joe Goodfield (7) 65
Aaliyah Morris (7) 65
Alix Mortier (7) 66
Romeo Barr (8) 66
Millie Wildego (7) 66
Samuel Frederick (8) 67
Sid Gilbert (7) 67
Kittie Mae Hastings (10) 67
Anika Vajagic (9) 67
Michael Akintoye (9) 68
Jade Olusanya (9) 68
Bolanle Akinkunle (9) 68
Arbër Mehmeti (9) 68
Lauren Harper (9) 68
Kate Moses (9) 69
Holly Holding (9) 69
Emma Elsley (9) 69
Salimah Bah (9) 69
Lucy Holmes (9) 69
Yasmin Marcos (9) 70
Jazmin Nwosu-Ekpete (10) 70

St James Hatcham CE Primary School, New Cross
Rebecca Mukasa (10) 70
Enitoluwafe Adesile (9) 71
Oluwaseun Akinsiwaju (11) 71
Bayode Abass (8) 72

St Luke's CE Primary School, Islington
Bachir Moujahid (8) 72
Kimberly Onen (9) 73
David Tabala (8) 74
Ronni-Rose Rowland (8) 75
Amie O'Connor (9) 75
Joshua Guy (9) 76
Fatjona Palushi (10) 77
Ellis Harris (9) 78
Islam Muhammed Kadri (10) 78
Mustafa Kidher (8) 79
George Petters (8) 80
Jacob Donaldson (9) 80
Sakina Buhari (8) 81
Micah Agyen (10) 81
Jay Gallacher (9) 82
Olamide Johnson (8) 83
Diana Curejova (9) 84
Fahim Muhammad Miha (8) 85
Kyron Wong (8) 86
Edvin Cai (9) 87
Rajon Deb (9) 88
Rebecca Matthews (9) 89
Emmanuella Ankrah (8) 90
Chloe Lewis (9) 91
Muhammad Buhari (8) 92
Imran Islam (9) 92
Lewis Slater Horgan (8) 93
Jackie Opuku Appiah (9) 94
Ayman Chehab (9) 94
Kane Melton (9) 95
Dennis Dincer (10) 95
Shihab Hussain (8) 96
Sara Tabala (10) 96
Harry Eaton (10) 97
Rozerin Edebali (10) 97
Mia Bassett (8) 98

Riyad Kahir (10) 98
Chloe Zambon (9) 99
Sinead Hannon (9) 99
James Gallacher (8) 100
Tia Harrold (9) 100
Ruhani Nwaka Eggay Muhammad (10).. 101
Ellie Sutherland (10) 101
Judah Olajide (9) 102
Sam Orgill (10) 102
Madiha Islam (10) 103
Awa Conteh (9) 103
Emily Hold (9) 104
Fiona Cunningham (9) 104
Cheryl Gill (9) 104
Dylan Lubo (10) 105
Rashaan Stewart (9) 105

St Mary of the Angels RC School, Bayswater
Loren Pacarada (9) 106
Abel Zemed (10) 107
Matteo Savant (8) 108
Cibelle Alves Harb (9) 109
Sam Gébler (9) 109
Michael Mendoza (8) 110
Roya (8) 110
Skye Matthew-Casu (9) 111
Uroliss Mendes (10) 111
Fareedah Shardow (10) 112
Thiyana Nurse (10) 112
Oliver Carino (9) 113
Ines Guerra-Riola (10) 113
Michaela Da Silva (7) 114
Nicolle Mendoza (10) & Rayna Lavado .. 114
Joshua Padpu (11) 115
Luca Martinez Freitas (10) 115
Anabela Soares (9) 116
Alice Lucchini 116
Yassin Akhatar (10) 117
Simonpietro Magrelli (9) 117
Sara Lacanale (11) 118
Brando Kennedy (10) 118
Joana Da Silva (9) 119
Michou Lutete (9) 119
Oliviero Kelly (7) 119

Adam Desouza (10) 120
Tiana Lacanale (8) 120
Charlene Della (8) 120
Flynn Ryan (9) 121
Grace McKenna (10) 121
Tommaso Kelly (7) 121
Micah Ashe (11) 122

St Thomas More RC Primary School, Eltham
Karen Bannor (10) 122
Danielle Omoregbee (10) 123
Nicole Ozborne (8) 123
Daniel Truss (11) 123
Sharleen Nkwo (10) 124
Isabella Vargas (10) 124
Leon Mann (9) 124
Della Sargeant (11) 125
Brandon-Jo Neale 125
Jack Sargeant (11) 125
Emily Shorter (11) 126
Michael Omoregbee (8) 126
Molly Fitzpatrick (11) 126
Ted Hepburn (10) 127
Francesca Aseoche (8) 127

Timbercroft Primary School, Plumstead
Georgia-Rose Beahan (11) 127
Shannon Bell (10) 128
Alfie Taylor (10) 128
Erin Hambly (10) 129
Tariq Ameer (10) 129
Pallvi Goutam (11) 130

Upton Cross Primary School, Plaistow
Shahir Ali (10) 130
Maisha Hussain (9) 131
Nishat-Ara Ali (9) 132
Yusuf Bobat (9) 133
Ayesha Kamran (10) 134
Thira Ul-Haq (9) 134
Adham Chaudhary (10) 135
Hassan Hussain (10) 135
Bilal Qureshi (10) 136
Taneem Kirbria (9) 136

Maryam Ahmed (9) 137
Abdullah Patel (9) 137
Razaool Haque (9) 137

Wormholt Park Primary School, Shepherd's Bush
Hannah Rockett (11) 138
Abdirizak Ali (10) 138

Wyborne Primary School, New Eltham
Patrick Ukagba (9) 138
Owen Phelps (9) 139
Conor Shiels (9) 139
William Guest (9) 140
Thomas Miller (8) 140
Molly-Rose Heselden (8) 141
Ella Hale (9) 141
Benjamin Luxford (8) 142
Luke Hazelton (9) 142
Subeeksha Jeyasangar (8) 143
Taylor Hollman (8) 143
Tunmishe Moronwiyan (8) 144
Vinnie French-Gibbens (8) 144
Ella'mai Aldridge (8) 145
Sophie Luckett (8) 145
Chloe French (9) 146
Anumita Mukherjee (9) 146
Sydney Cammiss-Brown (9) 147
Louie Cameron (8) 147
Lydia Hackwood (8) 148
Oliver Hayhoe (9) 148
Luke Redburn (9) 149
Eric Bui (9) 149
Saleh Ali (9) 149
Kirat Singh Chana (9) 150
Diante Grant (8) 150
Sam Bennett (8) 150
Kelly Delohery (9) 151
Sachin Thorogood (8) 151
Elise Hodson (9) 151
Tommy Delohery (9) 151
Leila McQuillen (9) 152
Max Morton (8) 152
Luke Ogunbameru (8) 152
Jaiden Ismond (8) 152

Mia Bennett (9) 153
Sandra Jacek (9) 153
Muhammed Ali Gunebakan (8) 153

The Poems

The Evacuee

Hurriedly she dragged me,
Speechlessly I walked.
Trying not to cry,
Trying not to talk.

Slowing me down,
Making me frown.
My dusty old suitcase,
That's all that I carry around.

Questions in my mind,
I ignore and leave behind.
So to the station we went,
To my destiny I am being sent.

Now we are here,
As from her eye there comes a tear.
Putting my two hands on her cold wet cheeks,
My body terrified as it slowly grows bleak.

She's hugging me now,
Hugging me tight.
She's closing her eyes,
Her tense face filled with lies.

Pulling me up and onto that train,
There's a lump in my throat as I can't stand the pain.

We're ripping apart now,
She's turning away.
Her face paler than pale,
Tears flooding down her face.

My mother crying,
My mind swirling.
Was this a dream?
For into my fate I am curling.

Shelby Tayab Dosdos (10)
All Souls CE Primary School, Westminster

The Shootout

Pant, pant.
I'm sweating.
I place the ball on the dot.

The others stand behind the line.
It's the World Cup.
The fans scream my name.

If I score I'll be famous.
I can't miss.
I'm determined to score.

I distance myself.
I aim for my left.
I take a deep breath.

My head
Aches
And aches.

The whistle goes.
I see my fame flash before my eyes.
I run.

I kick.
The fans scream.
My teammates hug me.

The opponents weep in defeat.
I later receive my medal.

Theo Turan (10)
All Souls CE Primary School, Westminster

My Unicorn

I gaze up at the midnight sky
I see her, my unicorn, galloping through the midnight sky
I think of her white fur and gold horn
She watches over me as I sleep
I dream I'm riding her through a forest of goblins feeling her fur
They say, 'Look at that boy riding through the forest so gracefully.'
Then I wake up, it is morning, she is gone
But I will see her tonight.

Immanuel Ogendo (10)
All Souls CE Primary School, Westminster

ONCE UPON a RHYME 2011 – London

The Evacuee

Each tearful mother, full of devastation, still as a statue, tries to swallow the lump in her throat.
Every stern father, helmet on head, keeping their battered chin up, and muddy fingers crossed hoping for victory.
Clueless children, whispering over the commotion, pale faces getting paler and paler by the second, waiting for the steam train to arrive as they blink hard, allowing the tears to trickle down.
Melancholy and misery fill their hearts at the sight of worn-out children, standing on the ruins of a cathedral, turned into rubble.
The old tatty bags, full of memories, good and bad, sway back and forth tucked tightly in a child's side.
Her rubbery mask, full of stench, protectively kept in the cardboard box, swings along with its string attached, as the child takes steps towards the carriage doors.
Normal family life turned into a living nightmare, made from hell, in a matter of hours, all from a speech from the prime minister.
Puffs of cloudy smoke steam out of the black dirty funnel as it drifts away into the distance.
More and more babies wail and whine from the cold, sinking through the home-made blanket.
As the children spread tears across the train carriage, pouring out, unable to keep in.
Everyone waves and doesn't stop.

Alison Weaver (10)
All Souls CE Primary School, Westminster

The Evacuee

Eyes watering, I was overcome with fear.
Her consistent smile, I knew was false.
Her trembling hands touched my shoulders, as I caught her mood.
Her eyes, once twinkling, now as if they would burst.
My face filled with confusion as I tried to comfort my mother.
Rushing to school, we became surrounded by an air of melancholy.
The grey smoke of sorrow climbed into the mothers' eyes.
Her laugh, once filled with joy, now a broken glass scattered across the floor.
Trapped inside the prison, watching my mother gradually fade as the steaming monster pulled from the station.

Cleah Black (10)
All Souls CE Primary School, Westminster

My Evil Hamster

I saw my evil hamster steal a ring
I saw a criminal as pale as snow
I saw the moon roll down the Earth
I saw a ball eat a chicken burger
I saw a man go to school
I saw a kid tell off a teacher
I saw a headmaster wear a nappy
I saw a baby who knows his times tables
I saw a junior bite a cage
I saw my evil hamster

I saw a ship roll down fire
I saw a rock write a story
I saw a child explode with lava
I saw a volcano clean clothes
I saw a washing machine do a handstand
I saw a gymnast

I saw the king kill a person
I saw Jack the Ripper eat human flesh
I saw a killer dog talk
I saw a man fly
I saw a bird do one of his evil plans
I saw my evil hamster.

Sameer Wahid (10)
All Souls CE Primary School, Westminster

The Evacuee

Trapped underneath the terror, she packed.
Holding a forced smile, the box was slung over my shoulder.
The train noise echoed through my mind.
I knew it was getting ready to drive into the distance.
Her pale skin glistened as tear after tear filled her sorrowful eyes.
The sound of the train signalled the children's unknown journey.
As the train pulled away from the station I counted every last step as she walked away.
My heart broke as the surrounding children anxiously discussed their unknown journey.

Ellie Simmons (10)
All Souls CE Primary School, Westminster

Once Upon a Rhyme 2011 – London

The Evil, Dark School

On a corner of a scorching, sparkling street
Stands a dark, gloomy, horrible school
The pitch-black gates surround the entire noisy school
And broken see-saws outrun by ants
And a tiny slide is left untouched
A mysterious boy is standing in the centre
Of this so-called chaos
His beautiful eyes are filled with freezing water
His soft hand
Zing
And
Zang

Here in the heart of the school is the dining room
All the food is sweet and tasty
The dinner ladies are kind
And would not take no for an answer
You can eat cold ice cream
And delicious fruit
When a new child comes
Welcome him
Welcome him
Welcome him.

Eyasin Ali (10)
All Souls CE Primary School, Westminster

Tudor Whipping Boy

What an awful day at school with the master's whipping
How I wish that boy can be
Extra good for me
I have a bruised back which is purple, blue and yellow
And no matter what, I always hate that fellow
I go back to the naughty boy
When he brings out a toy
Then he shows some joy when . . .
Whack
Whack
Whack
Here I am with a bruised back.

Raania Hammoudan (9)
All Souls CE Primary School, Westminster

The Evacuee

Hot tears pouring down my snow-white cheeks.
Bending my head my curls cascade down my face.
Speechless with emotion and dread,
Little hands holding bigger, trying to hold on forever,
Never letting go.

Other hands grasping brown paper bags
With the few precious belongings they cannot part with.
Holding on to worn out teddies,
Their heads laid upon their mothers' warm laps.

As the train pulls away steam bellowing out of its funnel,
Children banging frantically against the glass windows.
Steamed with their tears,
Mothers' hands still held up in farewell,
Watching the train fly away
Until it's a tiny steaming dot in the distance.

As people walk away,
Mothers stumble,
Not believing that their baby is gone from them.

Lily Pearce (11)
All Souls CE Primary School, Westminster

The Funny Penguin

On a hot summer's day in London Zoo
I saw a penguin looking at me
He did a funny dance that made me laugh
The zookeeper had no idea at all
He was the cutest thing
I wish I could take him home

It was the most fantastic thing
I told my mum I named him Cookie
I loved him lots and lots
When he stopped dancing he was like a monkey
I wish I could take him home

He never ever made you sad
There was such a great and fabulous feeling in me
I wish I could take him home.

Nell Cronin (9)
All Souls CE Primary School, Westminster

Sweetie Wonderland

When I'm walking
Through the sand
I know I'm in a wonderland
It's full of sweets
I love those treats
And it's full of peace.

It smells fresh, it tastes warm
I love its form
I hear the Haribo orchestra
Singing a tune until noon.

I feel the warm breeze
On my knees
And at least I can see
The sea under the tree.

I smell the sweet marshmallows
In the meadow with the mellow
Peace of silence.

Daniella Pollendine (10)
All Souls CE Primary School, Westminster

Snow

It was a trembling day
Nothing to say
All alone in the cold
Not doing as I was told
The birds were cold on the tree
'Cause there was a lot of breeze
It was like the world was frozen
Everyone was shivering
'Cause the land was like ice
Suddenly came a storm
Boom
Boom
Boom.

Sharika Ahmed (9)
All Souls CE Primary School, Westminster

Walking Into Light

My first scene in a new world,
A beautiful, magnificent, adorable light,
Shining in my mother's eyes so bright,

I twist and turn to make myself comfortable,
But then in the end I look so lovable,

People all around me smiling at me,
But then a sec later they look so scary,

Please, please, Mother help me,
These people are really, really freaky,

Yep I know I'm just a baby,
But I don't know how I wrote this poem,

My mum said I will walk in a year,
But two years later, I'm still not walking,

This is a poem about my life,
Thanks.

Leo Blanchet (10)
All Souls CE Primary School, Westminster

The Evacuee

Helplessly, I watched frantic hands pack my possessions.
A single tear trickled down her cheek.
I could see through her false smile.
Silently, she carried me through the tears of everyone.
Carefully, without looking back, I stumbled onto the train.
The mothers in the background bravely trying to hold their tears.
Steam poured out of the funnel and the train was on its way.
She kept waving her hands until it had carried me away.

Tife Adegbemile (10)
All Souls CE Primary School, Westminster

Shadows

Shadows, shadows, they are so frightening
At dark midnight
They come when there is lightning.

It hides in the darkness
It comes out at light
It vanishes at dead midnight.

When I turn around it gives me a scare
Wherever I go it follows me everywhere.

Shadows, shadows, they are so frightening
At dark midnight
They come when there is lightning.

When I turn around it gives me a scare
But I have to know it has to stay there.

S-h-a-d-o-w-s
Shadows they make me so depressed.

Jake Brindle (10)
All Souls CE Primary School, Westminster

The Evacuee

The sour taste of destiny lingers, in every heart and soul,
A sea of confused faces that look much like my own.
All thoughts are on those far away, fighting for their children every day.

I clutch the hand that cares for me,
Since I was born and began to be.
To save these precious moments she fights,
Amongst the screams and fading lights.

Cutting through the chaos, a beacon of bravery signals the end,
The pain and misery is becoming a trend.

I scream for my mother, one last try,
If she does not notice me, I'm bound to cry.
Her eyes are blurred by tears,
Her face answers my fears.

The sour taste of destiny lingers, in every heart and soul,
As we surge forward into the unknown.

Kira Miller (11)
All Souls CE Primary School, Westminster

The Serpent Gorgon

Yo king don't marry my mother
If you do I'll get an unwanted brother.
I'll do any task
I'll even wear a mask.

OK, OK, tomorrow when you get out of bed
Bring me back Medusa's bleeding head.
I want you to kill her nice and quick
And after that give her a flick.

This will be like killing a bee
Medusa won't do anything to me.
Hey look there's Athene
Everyone says she's a big fat meanie.

Maybe I was wrong, she gave me a shield
Now I think she's helping me fight in the battlefield.
Hey there's Hermes holding a sword
I think he is a real lord.

I found Medusa in her cave
And then I said you're going to your grave
I cut her head off nice and quick
And then I gave it a little flick.

Anastasia Theodorou (10)
Barclay Primary School, Leyton

Creeping

Creeping through
The dark and endless corridor
Of palace peace

Breaking the silence
Gentle sounds
Of thudding
Footsteps.

Ashutosh Khatri (10)
Barclay Primary School, Leyton

Creatures, Beasts And Monsters

There are creatures,
That kill,
That slaughter,
And take

There are beasts,
That ruin,
That want,
And destroy

There are monsters,
That hate,
That lie,
And cheat

These creatures,
These beasts,
These monsters,
Are earthlings,
And humans,
Slash humanity.

Saarah Hossany (10)
Barclay Primary School, Leyton

A Giggle

One giggle got me
In trouble.
One giggle found my
Sense of humour.
One giggle couldn't
Stop.
One giggle turned
Into a laugh.
One giggle got
Me in detention.
One giggle never
Stopped.
Until it was just
A laugh.

Darren Kaj (10)
Barclay Primary School, Leyton

Poems

Some poems make you happy
Some make you cry
Some poems are really long
And some make you sigh
Some are really boring
And some are not
Some make you laugh
Some have the whole lot
Some are really interesting
And some are about bath time
Some have no pictures
And some are like a clock chime
There are many poems
So don't be bored
You can read them all
So don't be a fraud!

Wissam Nahi (10)
Barclay Primary School, Leyton

Sea Poetry

The sea is an enormous lake,
Where people go to have a break.
The biting crabs, the crashing waves,
Whenever I go there I have to behave.
Because the lovely sea can be very angry,
Swallowing your body when it's hungry.
So do be careful next time you go,
Because now it's time for me to end this rhyme
By leaving you alone.

Mariam Olusunmade (10)
Buxton School Primary Phase, Leytonstone

The Highwayman
(Inspired by 'The Highwayman' by Alfred Noyes)

The wind was a torrent of darkness among the gusty trees.
The moon was a ghostly galleon tossed upon cloudy seas.
I came riding, riding across the purple moor
And then I met face to face with the old inn door.

I had a three cornered hat, and a bunch of lace at my chin.
A coat of crimson velvet and breeches of black cow skin.
They fitted without a crease and they were also up to the thigh!
My eyes were full of twinkles, my rapier glistened under the jewelled sky.

I went to my true love Bess,
Who was wearing a beautiful dress.
And I said, 'One kiss my bonny sweetheart!
I'm after a prize tonight!
I will be back with the sparkling gold before the morning light.'

For moments I went and then came back but Bess was all tied up!
She took a deep breath and then shattered her breast to warn me it was a trap.
I went ballistic and I only wanted revenge!
Revenge! Revenge! Revenge!
All I could think of was revenge!

I spurred like a madman, shrieking a curse to the sky.
With the white road smoking behind me and my rapier brandished high!
I galloped and clashed over the cobbles for I got shot in my heart
And then I died right there in the eerie dark . . .

Jonald Rakipaj (11)
Essendine Primary School, Maida Vale

The Highwayman
(Inspired by 'The Highwayman' by Alfred Noyes)

The wind was a torrent of darkness
Upon the gusty trees,
The moon was a ghostly galleon,
Tossed upon cloudy seas,
The road was a ribbon of moonlight,
Over the purple moor.

As I plaited a crimson love knot
Into my long black hair,
I heard that wonderful whistling sound
Far in the distance.
He'd boots up to his thigh and a twinkle in his eye,
As he rode under the jewelled sky.

There he was whistling a tune,
To tell me that he had arrived at last.
'One kiss my bonny sweetheart
I'm after a prize tonight
I shall be back with yellow sparkling gold

Watch me by moonlight
Look for me by moonlight
Though hell should bar the way.'

Suddenly King George's men held me by the hand,
My heart was a thumping drum.
My eye was a ball of fear
The highwayman's eyes were full of rage
So I knew that he was near.

My ghostly death was close.
My ghostly death was nigh.
I got tied near my bed
So I was not able to say goodbye.

The highwayman was coming
As my tears dropped to the ground.
I heard that lovely clatter
I heard that lovely sound.

King George's men came riding,
Riding to kill.
For us it was fear
For the men it was thrill.

One painful, hard shot.
And I dropped to the floor,
So the highwayman heard that sound, went running back
Went running over the purple moor.

I had told my ghostly tale
Now life has come to an end.
But will start again some day
But a ghost I shall send.
And nothing will get in the way.

Asil Ibrahim (11)
Essendine Primary School, Maida Vale

The Highwayman
(Inspired by 'The Highwayman' by Alfred Noyes)

Tlot! Tlot! Tlot!
I, the highwayman, galloped through
Over the ribbon of the moonlight the road was a dragon's tail.
I set eyes on my true love Bess,
I approached her with my horse,
My bonny sweetheart.

I am after a prize, a gold shivering necklace
Watch me by moonlight,
Call me by moonlight
I shall come with a prize possession for you.

I returned my bonny sweetheart
I have the shivering gold necklace
I galloped across the dark, eerie path
To get to be with my sweet love
I arrived at the inn door at the solid path
With a bird's-eye view I spotted my true love Bess
With red blood dripping out of her sweet mouth.

Rami Bettache (11)
Essendine Primary School, Maida Vale

The Highwayman
(Inspired by 'The Highwayman' by Alfred Noyes)

Once upon a rhyme . . .
As I was walking over the purple moors;
There was someone opening his inn yard doors.
When the moon turned into a ghostly galleon;
And my rapier glistening in the jewelled sky.
I heard a beautiful whistling from far away;
Which made me change my dearest way!

It was the landlord's daughter;
The landlord's black-eyed daughter;
She was Bess, plaiting a scarlet love knot into her long, silky hair.
There he was in the old inn yard, where a stable wicket creaked;
Where Tim the ostler, his face was nasty and peaked.
His eyes were hollows of madness . . .
But he loved the landlord's daughter.

I told Bess a secret meeting;
When someone stealthily moved;
But no one was able to be seen!
Off she went near the encasement.
Tim went and told the king.
Which gave the soldiers a humorous shock.

The sparkling black-eyed daughter.
Wasn't sure of what was happening.
I never came in the dawning;
I never came at noon; and not in the sunset!
She saw a troop of red clothes;
Where there was a violent attack;
They tied her up and locked her in the corner.

The strings were thick and strong;
Which meant there was no escape.
The tip of the finger touched it;
But she stayed calm at the moment.

Then I came riding;
Riding, riding.
Bess glanced at me like I was made from jewels and gold.
She warned me with her death.
Her own claret blood;
Laying on the floor.

There I was like a madman;
Shrieking a curse to the sky;
When they shot me down on the highway;
And this is how it ends.

Yassir Mahdi (11)
Essendine Primary School, Maida Vale

Bess

(Inspired by 'The Highwayman' by Alfred Noyes)

As I lay there in the darkness,
Under the jewelled sky.
I was waiting for my true love,
As the hours crawled by.

Finally, my true love came,
He kissed me on the cheek.
He said something to me,
That was really sweet.

'One kiss my bonny sweetheart,
I'm after a prize tonight.
I'll be gone the whole afternoon,
But I'll be back in the moonlight.'

He rode and rode away,
With his rapier and his gun.
I really, really hope,
That he will often run.

A colossal crowd came sprinting,
Sprinting towards me.
They came and grabbed my arms and legs,
And didn't set me free.

They tied me up from head to toe,
And tightened very hard.
I tried to cut my body free,
But beside me was a guard.

I tried to warn the highwayman,
So I picked up a big knife.
I stabbed myself in my crimson heart,
By the time it was morning light.

Dreni Muhaxheri (10)
Essendine Primary School, Maida Vale

The Highwayman
(Inspired by 'The Highwayman' by Alfred Noyes)

The wind was a cascade of darkness among the gusty trees,
The moon was a ghostly galleon sailing peacefully upon cloudy seas,
The road was white and twisted like a ribbon of moonlight
And I came riding, riding, riding,
Over the purple moor, up to the old inn door.

I'd a French cocked hat just covering my forehead,
A cluster of lace at my chin,
A coat of claret velvet and trousers of brown doe skin,
They fitted, fitted, with never a wrinkle, my boots were up to the thigh,
And I rode with a jewelled twinkle in my eye,
Under the jewelled sky.

I whistled a tune to the window,
And who should be waiting there,
Bess the landlord's daughter
With skin as white as snow and lips as red as blood,
Plaiting a dark red love knot in her long black hair.

'One kiss my bonny sweetheart, I'm after a prize tonight,
Yet if they press me sharply and hurry me through the day,
Then look for me by moonlight,
Watch for me by moonlight,
I'll come to thee by moonlight, though hell should bar the way.'

I did not come in the dawning, I did not come at noon
I did not come at sunset
But finally at the stroke of midnight.

Tlot-tlot, tlot-tlot in the frosty silence,
Tlot-tlot, tlot-tlot in the echoing night,
Over the ribbon of moonlight, echoing in the night,
I could see my true love, her face lit up like a light,
She drew one last breath and shattered her breast in the night.

I shrieked a curse to the sky,
King George's men had killed her,
I never thought that my true love Bess
Would ever actually die.

I took out my rapier,
And charged in the moonlight,
I knew I could never win,
But I could never live without my true love Bess,
And then the king's men shot me and I died right there in the moonlight.

Qamil Pajaziti (11)
Essendine Primary School, Maida Vale

The Highwayman
(Inspired by 'The Highwayman' by Alfred Noyes)

The moon was a ghostly galleon thrown upon cloudy seas,
The wind was a gust of darkness, among the gusty trees,
Over the ribbon of moonlight, over the purple moor,
I came galloping through the old inn's doors.

My rapier glinted under the jewelled night,
Whistling a tune, I signalled to my love that I was at sight.
Patiently waiting was Bess, with her silky hair near the windowpane,
Plaited was her dark hair enclosed with a scarlet love knot.
Her love for me was insane!

I scurried to my love and grasped her like a bear,
How I wish I could do this all day!
Told her I'd be back with bags full of gold; and put them there,
I'd be back by moonlight, though hell should bar the way!

Reluctantly I left my beloved one,
I rode away to the west.
Marching after me came the king's men,
To run away, I tried my best!

My love, from bed was uncovered,
My beloved, my weak point had been discovered!
There was death at every window!
All I could do was run . . .

Down the ribbon of moonlight, over the purple moor, riding, riding.
Until I heard the sound that I had dreaded.
Bang!
My true love. *Dead!*

Tasnima Islam (10)
Essendine Primary School, Maida Vale

The Highwayman
(Inspired by 'The Highwayman' by Alfred Noyes)

The moon rode on a wave of clouds,
As the stars waved hello.
The wind was a torrent of madness,
As the sky was as peaceful as midnight,
The road was a ribbon of madness,
As the leaves scattered along . . .

My face gallant and firm,
Riding on my mighty steed,
Galloping furiously as the yawning sun set behind me,
My mask absorbed into my skin,
Hiding my identity . . .

Over the rocks and cobbles I crumbled
Breaking into the old inn yard.
I tapped the shutter with my coal-black whip.
Nothing. All barred up and locked.

I whistled a tune to the window.
But who should be waiting there?
Bess, the landlord's daughter,
The sparkling black-eyed daughter.

As she let loose a red knot in her coal-black hair,
I planted a kiss on her red-lipped lips.
I whispered into her bonny ears,
'I'm after only one prize tonight!'
As I climbed on my steed I shouted,
'I'll be back my dearest love.'

Unfortunately my fortune was lost,
I smiled,
As I knew what my heart pounded for,

I arrived, once again at the old inn door,
I stopped, my eyes open wide
'Bess!' I screamed
But I knew she was gone.
My heart crushed as I felt a sharp pain,
I was shot!
My life was over without my love's desire . . .

Hanna Abdalla (11)
Essendine Primary School, Maida Vale

The Highwayman
(Inspired by 'The Highwayman' by Alfred Noyes)

The wind was a torrent of darkness,
The moon was a ghostly galleon,
The road was a ribbon of moonlight,
And there I saw my love.

Riding and riding,
With his twinkle in his eye.
His French cocked hat on his forehead
His skin as white as snow
And his rapier glistening underneath the jewelled sky.

'My love, I will be back in the morning light,
I'm after a prize tonight,' he said.
Tlot, tlot, tlot
And off my love went.

As the hours crawled by,
I was plaiting a crimson love knot into my dark hair.
King George's men came marching,
And captured me by the hand.

They left me with a gun behind me,
I knew they wanted the highwayman,
But I didn't want my love to die.
Then I saw him coming by.

I tried to stop him from coming,
I shot myself so I could warn him.
I saw the downhearted face he had.
He stopped and turned back
But I knew my love was going to die.

They shot him as he was riding back,
He lay on the floor,
With his crimson blood scattered everywhere.
I lay on the ground too.

The wind was a torrent of darkness,
The road was a ribbon of moonlight,
The moon was a ghostly galleon,
And there I saw my love.

Aishah Begum (10)
Essendine Primary School, Maida Vale

The Highwayman
(Inspired by 'The Highwayman' by Alfred Noyes)

The wind was a torrent of darkness among the gusty trees,
The stars glistened and reflected in the waving seas,
The trees swished and swirled across the moonlight,
It was very dark and I was out of sight.

I was wearing a French cocked hat lying on my forehead,
A coat of soft, claret velvet and breeches of brown doe skin,
My boots were up to my thigh,
And I rode with a jewelled twinkle in the middle of my eye.

Who should be waiting there?
Bess, the landlord's red-lipped daughter,
'One kiss my bonny sweetheart, I'm after a prize tonight,
So look for me by moonlight,
Watch for me by moonlight.'

Then I drifted away.
After I came back,
Bess wasn't waiting,
Red blood was all over her,
I rushed to them like a madman.

King George's men were there,
My horse went and ran,
King George's men all rushed me,
A sword came out of nowhere,
And then my life was over.

Ali Hussain (11)
Essendine Primary School, Maida Vale

The Highwayman
(Inspired by 'The Highwayman' by Alfred Noyes)

The wind was a torrent of darkness
Among the gusty trees,
Making a screeching sound,
But there was another whispering noise . . .
As I was waiting for my true love,
I was plaiting a scarlet love knot in my long black hair.

Tlot, tlot, tlot
The highwayman came riding, riding.
The highwayman came riding up to the old inn door.
As he said to me, 'One kiss my bonny sweetheart,
I am after a prize tonight.'

I was watching through my casement
For my true love to come riding through the moonlight.
The king's men came marching, marching,
The king's men came marching up to the old inn door.

I was tied up by King George's men,
Used as bait for my true love.
Tlot, tlot, tlot, my face grew pale.
I knew my true love would be caught . . .
Bang!

Here I am once again as my ghostly spirit,
Plaiting a dark ruby love knot in my long black hair.

Imaan Magou (10)
Essendine Primary School, Maida Vale

Bess
(Inspired by 'The Highwayman' by Alfred Noyes)

As I was waiting for my true love,
I heard a whistle outside my window.
I looked out my window and who could it be?
It was my fabulous man.
The highwayman told me something so sweet, it was . . .
'Look for me by moonlight,
Watch for me by moonlight,
I'll come to thee by moonlight,
Come though Hell should bar the way!'
He also whispered, 'One kiss my bonny sweetheart!'

Then quick as a blink he rode off.
Whilst I was plaiting my long black hair,
I heard *stamp, stamp, stamp!*
I looked out of my large window.
I was worried sick,
It was the evil army, the soldiers of King George.
The soldiers were on their way to my house.
I was in a bad fright.
They tied me up to my bed.
The army asked me questions about the highwayman!
But I didn't answer them.

Yassmine Fadley Mtiri (11)
Essendine Primary School, Maida Vale

Bess
(Inspired by 'The Highwayman' by Alfred Noyes)

Every time I look through the window
I ask myself, will he come back?
Does he love me?

I always imagine him galloping towards me
My heart aches when I think about him.

Could the highwayman be the one?
When I see him I can't stop my eyes from looking at the highwayman.

He says his speech then gallops away.
Will he come back?

Bronte Paul (10)
Essendine Primary School, Maida Vale

The Highwayman
(Inspired by 'The Highwayman' by Alfred Noyes)

The wind was a torrent of darkness among the gusty trees.
I came riding, riding.
My rapier glinted upon the jewelled sky,
With a twinkle in my eye.

Whilst whistling a fancy tune it drew attention to Bess, the landlord's daughter,
The landlord's black-eyed daughter.
Plaiting a dark scarlet love knot in her hair.
I told her, 'My bonny sweetheart, I'm after a prize tonight,
I shall be back by the morning light.'

As hours crawled by I went riding for my gold.
I heard sweet Bess' voice echoing through my head.
I rode with a delicate twinkle though Hell should bar the way.

I arrived a second too late as beautiful Bess had shot herself just for my love's refrain.
I turned; I spurred like a madman.
They shot me down on the highway.
Down like a dog on the highway.
And lay my blood on the highway.

Tahani Mahamud (10)
Essendine Primary School, Maida Vale

Highwayman
(Inspired by 'The Highwayman' by Alfred Noyes)

Tlot. Tlot. Tlot.
There was a man with a black mask,
A French cocked hat.
He was riding a white fluffy horse
To the old inn door.
His name was the highwayman.

As he arrived at the old crusty inn door,
His eyes opened wide as he saw a beautiful lady
Who was the landlord's daughter.
The brave masked man said,
'I will bring you a gold necklace.'

Muminul Islam (10)
Essendine Primary School, Maida Vale

The Highwayman
(Inspired by 'The Highwayman' by Alfred Noyes)

Tlot, tlot, tlot,
I, the highwayman, galloped
Over the ribbon of moonlight,
And under the cloudy skies,
The road was a dragon's tail,
I set eyes on Bess, my bonny sweetheart,
Waiting patiently looking out the casement.

My sharp rapier hung loose from my trousers,
And my pistol jewelled a twinkle under the bright moonlit sky.
I, the highwayman, set eyes on my love Bess.
'My love Bess I'll be back with yellow shimmering gold.'

Tlot, tlot, tlot,
I rode to the old inn door,
With the yellow shimmering gold,
Who's that I see . . . drenched with red blood?
Nooo! It might be my love.
Oh nooo! The king's men!
Kkshtah! Kkshtah! Nooo . . . (gunshots)

Billal Damouche (10)
Essendine Primary School, Maida Vale

The Highwayman
(Inspired by 'The Highwayman' by Alfred Noyes)

Tlot, tlot, tlot,
The highwayman came riding, riding, riding
The highwayman came riding
Through the ribbon of moonlight
Over the purple moor.

The moon was a ghostly galleon
Through the torrent of darkness.
As he was surrounded no fear shivered upon him
Because he ought to meet
The love of his life.

Tim the ostler heard
He was as dumb as a dog
He had a roaring flame inside him,
He would do anything to have Bess
Even if he had to kill the highwayman.

Artin Pacolli (10)
Essendine Primary School, Maida Vale

The Highwayman
(Inspired by 'The Highwayman' by Alfred Noyes)

The wind was a torrent of darkness, among the gusty trees.
The moon was a ghostly galleon, tossed upon cloudy seas.
The road was a ribbon of moonlight over the purple moor.

He had a claret velvet coat which twinkled and sparkled.
It stood out at night,
Everyone in the village thought it was bad but it's the highwayman.

He had a French cocked hat on his forehead
And a bunch of lace at his chin.
The highwayman went galloping, galloping, galloping
Towards the old inn door.

A beautiful lady came and said, 'I love you.'
And he said, 'I love you too but I can't,
I'm a thief, I'm the highwayman.'

The highwayman went riding, riding, riding
Upon the gusty trees.
He came to a window and whistled a tune,
(Tweet, twoo, tweet, twoo).

Eldin Hasanovic (10)
Essendine Primary School, Maida Vale

The Landlord's Daughter, Bess
(Inspired by 'The Highwayman' by Alfred Noyes)

The stars glinted brightly, amongst the moonlit sky.
The moon shone warmly as if it were going to cry.
As I looked out to the forest, in search of my one treasure,
I heard a sudden galloping noise and my heart filled with pleasure.

The cunning fox had come to me, to savour the taste of my love,
His hand rose up to point at me revealing a pearly glove.
And there he was, the highwayman, with his smile and crimson coat.
With jet-black boots up to his thigh and lace at his bony throat.

'I will be back!' he called out loud. 'I will be back for you!
If not now, if not midnight, then dawn it shall be too!'
My heart had been filled with happiness and joy,
From the highwayman himself!
I loved him for his love and care, not robbery nor his wealth.
He galloped off into the night as I went back to my room,
But as quick as a flash I heard a noise,
A noise of death and doom.

Nabila Hussain (10)
Essendine Primary School, Maida Vale

The Highwayman
(Inspired by 'The Highwayman' by Alfred Noyes)

I was riding on my fastest horse,
Going down the haunted road.
I was going to my wonderful Bess.
I said to her, 'Wait for me by moonlight,
Look for me by moonlight,
I will come to thee by moonlight,
Though hell should bar the way.'
I will bring a necklace
That would be shiny as the sun.

Tlot! Tlot! Tlot! I went to rob the rich.
I came back and saw someone drenched in blood
And thought it was Bess.
'Oh no,' I felt a pain.
On my back, like a dog biting me.
I felt faint coming.

Muhammad Abu Bakar (10)
Essendine Primary School, Maida Vale

The Highwayman
(Inspired by 'The Highwayman' by Alfred Noyes)

The wind was a torrent of darkness among the gusty trees.
As I came riding, riding, riding to the old inn door.
Bess, the lovely landlord's daughter, was waiting for me.
Her eyes were like diamonds.
She was waiting for me.
I went to catch a big prize
And give my Bess a surprise.

As I galloped to the old inn door.
Boom! The guns had warned me like never before.
Bess, the landlord's daughter, was lying dead
On the dusty floor.
I was angry!
Boom!

The wind was a torrent of darkness among the gusty trees.
As I came riding, riding, riding,
To the old inn door.

Albin Salihu (11)
Essendine Primary School, Maida Vale

The Highwayman
(Inspired by 'The Highwayman' by Alfred Noyes)

The stars glistened in the beautiful jewelled sky.
The bright moonlight dyed the road with a shining white light
As it twinkled in my dark brown eyes.
The hooves of my horse made a steady beat
As I tried to lower my feet.

I made a stop to my true love's casement
As I can say to you it wasn't in the basement.
I whistled a tune to say I was here.
She listened closely with her hair behind her ear.

There I stood on the hard grey ground,
I spoke a few words with my rapier down.
'I shall be back before morning light.
If not, look for me by moonlight.'
Then off I hurried towards the sacred moonlight.

Chidima Akopoazu (10)
Essendine Primary School, Maida Vale

If An Alien Came Around

If an alien came to your school,
Would you scream and jump with fright?
If he jumped into the pool,
Would your face go completely white?

And in my past,
He burst into the class,
When he did this terrifying thing,
The burglar alarm,
Started to ring.

He suddenly took me to space,
What would you do in this case?
I'd meet him,
But not if he looked dim.

Then the teacher,
She ran away,
And everyone shouted,
'Hooray, hooray.'

'Oh dear me,'
The teacher said,
'No more lessons today,'
So once again,
'Hooray, hooray.'

'What should we do teacher?'
'Oh I'm not sure,'
The alien told me,
He could get more.

So if an alien,
Came to your school,
Would you do this
Or act so cool?

Sarah Delabriere (10)
Heathfield House School, Chiswick

School

School is laughter, school is life
If you don't go you'll be strife
I really must say you really are dumb
If you don't go your brain will go numb

So please, so please
Go to school now

I must say you have to learn
So you need to go
You'll learn to write
Do sums and learn not to fight
What do you like?
I don't care
You have to do it all
How old are you?
Seven Miss

Then go to primary school
Go to school now
I really must say
No, no, I don't want to
But you have to!
You have no choice

I must say you have to learn
So you need to go
You'll learn to write
Do sums and learn not to fight
What do you like?
I don't care
You have to do it all.

Ella Hourican (7)
Heathfield House School, Chiswick

Telling Tales

'Boys hand in your homework
No excuses, lies or tales
I expect straight As
No Bs or Cs or fails!

Harry where is yours?
Now, now, please don't lie.'
'Well, the thing is, Mister . . .
'No! Don't even try!'

(But he did!)

'It got stuck in my knickers drawer,
As I got it my hand got jammed,
I took it out then bandaged it and, and, and . . .
Then a dog went and sneezed on it so I put it in the dryer,
Started cooking, it was next to me,
Somehow ended up in the fryer!
I fished it out and washed it with a sponge and soap,
Then it went all soggy (didn't know if I could cope!)

I went with it to France and it got stuck in a baguette,
Took it out and sighed so there was no need to fret,
Then when we came back my piece was almost done,
(Looking after this essay was really not much fun!)
But then it disappeared one day (oh no, what a shame!)
So you see Mister Brown it's really not me to blame!'

Evie White (11)
Heathfield House School, Chiswick

I Believe I Can Fly!

I believe I can fly, in the blue, blue sky!
Birds are all around me.
In the distance I can see the beautiful sea,
I believe I can fly in the blue, blue sky!

I'm over the seaside, wow what a view!
Lots of people,
I bet they're evil!
Oh look there is a beautiful white eagle!
I believe I can fly in the blue, blue sky.

Esther Chemla (9)
Heber Primary School, Southwark

Poor Boy Now, Millionaire Soon

There once was a boy called Jack
Who slept inside a woollen sack
He lived with his mum
Who always was glum
'What shall we do now?'
'We'll have to sell our cow.'
He sold it for things green
And he noticed they were beans
'I'll have to plant them,' he said
'In my brilliant vegetable bed.'
In the morning sky
It grew very high
He climbed to the top
And smashed a pot
He saw a castle
With a picture of a rascal
He saw some gold
And he went forward bold
He saw a massive man
Who was eating a flan
The giant was bald
Jack took the gold
He put a time bomb on the wall
I must say Jack was cool
The place went boom
It blew up every room
He went to his mum
And showed her some
Of the money he got
And she said, 'That's a lot!'

Ruben Bø Dower (11)
Heber Primary School, Southwark

The Summer Night

Fireflies shine in the darkness,
A warm dazzle of heat sways between the trees.
The sound of crickets echoes into the darkness,
The birds start singing, it must be morning.

Isaac St Louis (8)
Heber Primary School, Southwark

The Seasons

There's a story of seasons to be told
That starts in winter when it's cold
Christmas trees and snowy skies
Santa's reindeer and mince pies

After that we move to spring
Where nature's glory fully takes wing
Daffodils bloom
Daisies galore
You'll enjoy it to be sure

Hip! Hip! Hooray!
It's now summer
Holiday, beaches
That's no bummer

Autumn's next
The leaves do fall
Hedgehogs hibernate
In a ball
To the long days
We say goodbye
Now there's fireworks and a guy

Now the story has been told
It's back to winter and it's cold.

Georgia Muraszko (9)
Heber Primary School, Southwark

Polar Bear

Kings and queens of the frozen north
They are family with the grizzly bear
Watch out! Arctic foxes
Watch out! Arctic seals!

They're spies on ice
They're also the
World's best hunters
They have the warmest fur too
Kings and queens of the frozen north
Polar bear.

Myles Williams (9)
Heber Primary School, Southwark

Saviour

There you lay
In the grave
Take a rest
You worked hard
At saving us all

You think you fought
For just naught
But you did much more
You saved the young
You saved the old

You saved the weak
Even the bold
You're our saviour
Oh yes you are

There you lay
In the poppy fields
As the wind
Slowly builds

You say
Goodbye
We say
Thank you.

Marika Ryan (10)
Heber Primary School, Southwark

Flowers

Flowers blooming in the sun
I think flowers are such fun
Different shapes under a sky so blue
Different colours for me and you
Pink for Crystal
Yellow for Sam
Blue for Dad
And purple for Mam.

Samantha Dobson (9)
Heber Primary School, Southwark

Realms

I'm a traveller:
First, I'm taking a stroll watching fire-elves and water-nymphs play.
Next, I'm with a party of ogres, but I don't want to stay.
Now, I'm in a haunted castle, the tell-tale stairs creaking underneath me.
Wait! I'm on Long John Silver's ship and pirates are teaching me how to sword fight.

Suddenly I'm knocked off my feet; I can feel sand beneath me.
The roaring of waves tells me I'm by the sea.
But I don't have time to linger . . .
Now I'm in Venice, the beautiful floating city.
I dive into the Grand Canal and start swimming with mermaids.

Their hair is matted seaweed.
Their sinuous tails . . . drenched in blood.
They are not mermaids at all anymore.
They are the fearsome vampire eels who swarm at the time of the flood.

I get pulled right down under the waves and as I lie on the sea bed,
I am also lying at the foot of my own bed.
I am filled with a peculiar sense of dread.
Have I returned or am I still there instead?

Isabel Nelson (10)
Heber Primary School, Southwark

She

She ran, I followed.
She told me not to but I didn't care.
I followed her anyway.
She told me it was dangerous.
I still went with her.
She squeezed under a metal fence.
It was sharp.
I watched her striped pyjamas,
Flapping in the wind.
She ran into a hut,
I turned away.
It happened to her,
What happened to them all.

Ella Pound (10)
Heber Primary School, Southwark

Three Little Pigs

There were once three little pigs
Who were bald and wore wigs
They built some houses of rock and twig
During this they all lost a wig,
The word they were all afraid of began with B
Whenever they heard it they went ooo-eee
The word they were afraid of was bacon
Because in the future it was forsaken,
Then the big bad wolf came along
His teeth were so awfully long
Then old wolfie began to feel
That he had not yet had a decent meal,
Then he saw three juicy pigs skipping along the path
Wolfie saw that they would make a decent meal and a half
He turned them into bacon and sausage
At least they came with no costage,
But he still felt that he was hungry
He thought he might go on holiday,
But he still felt that he was hungry
He thought he might go on holiday to Hungary.

Jayden Neil-White (11)
Heber Primary School, Southwark

My Fox

I have a fox,
Who chews my socks
No one knows
He lives in a box

I have a fox,
Who chews my socks
Who was caught in a rope
With difficult knots

I have a fox,
Who chews my socks
He bit a wire
And received five shocks.

Jay Hailstone Collier (10)
Heber Primary School, Southwark

Do Not Venture Deep And Dark

I have arrived, not a soul in sight
Everything is giving me a fright
The wood seemed to howl with the rustling trees
Waiting for what it please
I knew I could not run, I could not hide
But many people may have died
Venturing through these woods
Snakes hissed, bears growled
I was not proud
For this is where I have run
Not any trace of any fun
I crept and crawled curious of
What will happen next
Every heartbeat counted as my best
For I may die on this journey
Through the wood of hell
Do not run away from home
You may end up on your own!

Elizabeth Linke (8)
Heber Primary School, Southwark

The Spooks Next Door . . .

Two weeks ago some strange people moved in . . .
No one saw a delivery truck drive over,
No one saw any people,
All they saw was a sky-blue light and children peering
Through the crack of the door . . .
There wasn't an adult in sight,
The estate agent popped over to say, 'Hello!'
And now he is gone,
Then we got a note that seems to glow,
To go over for tea,
Should we go?

Ruairidh Higgins (9)
Heber Primary School, Southwark

Rushing Of The Waves

Waves, waves, I hear the waves
Children swimming
People surfing

Boats rustling to the wind
I hear the sea angry as could be
The waves are trying to catch me

Waves, waves, I hear the waves
Smash, crash, ahhh
At least, someone, try to help me!

Swirling round and round even faster . . .
I'm getting very dizzy
I see a lighthouse, I try to swim
But the waves are pulling me down
Like a sea monster . . .

So believe me please
It's a very big sea!

Tyan Benjamin (9)
Heber Primary School, Southwark

Teachers

T he teachers are always shouting in the staffroom.
'E at your dinner or you will be sick,' yelled Miss Burns.
'A lways keep your thinking hat on,' says Miss Platt.
C lass, be sensible, it's no time to joke about.
'H elp, I need help, Miss Kleywegt,' said Grace.
'E m, it's playtime, Miss. Can we go now?'
R ecess, it's recess, ring, ring, ring.
S chool is over, it's home time!

Victoria Adeyeye (9)
Heber Primary School, Southwark

Fields

Soft lush grass,
Swaying in the breeze,
Cows mooing,
And doing as they please,

Fields in the middle of nowhere,
Really hard to find,
Sun so bright,
Shining in your eyes,

Wild flowers,
Growing here and there,
A shadow,
As big as a bear,

A small broken cottage,
Tumbling down a path,
A small, cute kitten,
Wanting a bath.

Ruby Redman (9)
Heber Primary School, Southwark

Witches

Witches, witches
Where are they?

Are they sleeping
In the hay?

Witches, witches
Where are they?

Are they swimming
With a ray?

Witches, witches
Where are they?

Are they going to
Come and play?

Are they getting a hotel
Or somewhere to stay?

Chloe Sanguyu Harris (9)
Heber Primary School, Southwark

Miss Fig

Most teachers are boring,
Most teachers are glum,
But I know a teacher called Miss Fig,
Who is so much fun!

You're lucky if you get Miss Fig,
She'll fill you up with joy,
She's sure to make you laugh out loud,
She likes every girl and boy.

Her lessons are fantastic,
There's always things to learn,
Just like last week in history,
I learnt to use a churn.

What can I say about Miss Fig?
She always wants to play.
She'll put a smile on your face
And keep it there all day.

Louisa Underhill (9)
Heber Primary School, Southwark

Trapped Tiger

I was in heaven,
But now in hell.
This torture chamber is cold, damp and extremely dark!
Slowly turning white, my camouflaged fur is falling out.
Life flashes back before me,
The smell of death within my cage.
Why do I feel like a bunch of pet cats?
I long for relatives in vain,
Where every day is exactly the same.

Six paces left, six paces right,
That's all I get to do in my little tiger cell.
I'll hope I'll be set free to my wildlife kingdom.
I hope these cruel people get the sack.

I'm a tiger that is caged.
I wish to be free
And not in rage!

Louis Ashley-Brown (11)
Horn Park Primary School, Lee

Tortured Tiger

Hell!
I must be in Hell!
This torture chamber is cold
Dark
Extremely damp.
Slowly turning white,
My toasty fur
Falling out.

The dull air smells of death,
I feel like a pet cat:
Imprisoned.
I long for my family, in vain,
Every day is the same.

Will I ever be put back?
I hope these cruel people
Get the sack.
I take paces,
Not steps
Thinking . . .
What will I be next?

A fur coat?
A rug?
A doormat or a
Dreamcatcher?

I sigh . . .
I slump . . .
I cry . . .
Wondering . . .
Why?

Emily Ashcroft (11)
Horn Park Primary School, Lee

The Helpless Whales

We live in a paradise
But that's what baby whales think.
Next thing you know all whales are extinct.
We live in the sea
And swim happily.

Until the killer men come
They take their big nets
And catch every one.
Fish to fish
They know they will make an excellent dish.

One day I was swimming with my dad
Remembering all those fish which made me sad.
A net came down
I quickly turned around.
I looked for my dad
He was in the net.
Now that made me mad.

I got to the surface
But it was too late.
My dad could not breathe.
The killer men pulled and heaved
It was my life or his
It wasn't a decision.
I knew right from wrong
And I was right
I took a last sight
At the pretty sea
Gasping for air
Oh, silly me.

Philips Obakpolor (10)
Horn Park Primary School, Lee

Bear On The Wall

Bear, bear, on the wall,
What did you do to deserve to be in the hall?
Where is your body?
All I can see is your head.
I am afraid I don't want to be dead!
I see your eyes so black and small,
I want to cry but I don't want to be a fool.
Do you remember being free?
Now you're trapped like a bee.
Poor, poor you, upon the wall,
Are you not scared that you'll fall?
Are you big or are you small?
I really don't want you upon my wall.
You make me cry!
You make me sob!
You make me feel a little odd.
On the floor, here I lay,
Where your tears form a giant pool.
Full of guilt and despair,
Were you tortured or was your owner fair?
I can't imagine being in your shoes,
Going through all the pain and sorrow!
I can't imagine how your family feels,
Losing a sibling, a child or a friend.
I hope I meet a bear in person,
Only one and I will be happy.
Brown fur turning red like a fire,
Keeping us warm in bed.
Bear, bear, on the wall,
What did you do to deserve to be in the hall?

Kasey Bullen (11)
Horn Park Primary School, Lee

Trapped Tiger

I was in heaven,
But now in hell,
1, 2, 3, 4,
Paces to the door,
1, 2, 3, 4,
Paces back,
I'm a trapped tiger!

I was in heaven,
But now in hell,
My precious dreams are gone,
To live in the wild is gone,
And now I'm full of rage,
I'm a trapped tiger.

I was in heaven,
But now in hell,
Trapped by men forever,
What am I here for?
A rug, a lovely dish or a trophy,
I'm a trapped tiger.

I was in Heaven,
But now in Hell,
1, 2, 3, 4,
Paces to the door,
1, 2, 3, 4,
Paces back
Because I'm a trapped tiger!

Ahmet Akis (11)
Horn Park Primary School, Lee

Tiger, Tiger

Tiger, tiger, scared to death
All alone in a cage is left
Colossal cat with not much space
He is squished up right to his face

Tiger, tiger, biting steel
Wounds inside are hard to heal
There is no way out, no escaping out
He's trying to shout

Tiger, tiger, with bloody claws
Scratching old, beaten, rotten floors
Held by chains to keep him down
Everyone sees the frown

Tiger, tiger, catching your breath
Coming really near to your death
Crawling to the back of the cage
Coming to your breath of age.

Shauna Millard (11)
Horn Park Primary School, Lee

Tiger Poem

Dying in solitary pain,
Hearing the echoes of the train.

Fearful tiger brought to death,
They are trying to gain their breath.

Gaze at people who trapped him still
It's the tiger needing a water refill
As people gaze back, like watching a film.

Tiger, tiger, turning white,
Put down in a cage twice your height,
No life, no dignity.

Held by a chain in a hostile cage,
Nowhere for it to release its rage.

Once was smart and tremendously big,
But moving bent, bruised and wanting to die.

Loveshan Selvarajah (10)
Horn Park Primary School, Lee

Restless Cheetah

Fast like a motorbike
Now restless like a sloth
Not even a bit of a fat filling feast
I'm taken from my beloved family
I run through the grass
Bashing my paws on the glass
They all cheer
But do they hear?
My roar of terror
Putting me in this zoo was an error!
My claws are growing with rage
Is this the end of my story
Because there is no next page!
Is my life over?
Will I see outside?
Because this is my life.

Morgan Spencer (10)
Horn Park Primary School, Lee

Rhino

Rhino, rhino, locked away,
Nothing to do, not even play.
It's nearly the end,
The end of my life,
I feel like my heart's been struck by a knife.

Rhino, rhino, in a zoo,
Laughing at me, that's all they do.
Those people with their flashes bright,
It's my only glimpse of light.

Rhino, rhino, running free,
That's only a memory now for me.
On the plains, black and grey,
Return me to my home one day!

Arry Downey (11)
Horn Park Primary School, Lee

The Wasteful Whale

Her skin is as black as the night
You know we can save her, you and I.
Her eyes shimmer like a thousand stars
As she speeds through the sea like a racing car.

The biggest queen in the ocean
My heart broke as she made me feel emotion
Motionless blinks as she struggles through the net

Slaughter awaits as she swims towards her doom
Unseen fate in the watery gloom
Slashing, cutting, killing
She could have been very filling.

Rebecca Cladingboel (10)
Horn Park Primary School, Lee

Bear, Bear!

Bear, bear, everywhere,
I'm a tortured little bear,
I dance and dance till I have to stop,
I'm a poor, poor little bear.

The bears dance and dance till the owner has money,
Horrible, horrible, horrible, horrible,
Owner with the money.

I used to like the owner,
Till he didn't have any money.
I am tortured, tortured, tortured, tortured,
Little, funny bear.

Caris Toomer-Willis (10)
Horn Park Primary School, Lee

The Dancing Bear

Struggling in dreadful pain
A bear captured and held by chains.

Feeling lonely, feeling sad
Sitting there helplessly mad.

Everyone thinks it's a joke
But around your neck the chain chokes.

Swollen back legs bruised from prancing
Battered, beaten, make sure he's dancing.

His jaundiced eyes for help are pleading
Night and day his wounds are bleeding.

Jordan Ellis-Campbell & Rebekah Ahmed (10)
Horn Park Primary School, Lee

Tiger! Tiger!

Claustrophobic, locked up tight,
Seconds, hours, day and night.

Growing old, starting to age,
Boring life inside a cage.

Tiger! Tiger! Sitting still,
Crying out, wanting to kill.

Dreaming of forever free,
The wild really was for me.

Fading camouflage on my face,
No kill, no stripes, I have no space.

Adam Wiggins (11) & Ben Carberry (10)
Horn Park Primary School, Lee

Trapped

No luck for our furry friend,
His mighty mane is dropping low.
Steel bars surround him,
He misses his home,
The trees, the leaves, gone forever.

His life is at a halt,
Frightening teeth and terrible claws,
Mean nothing now!
Running, chasing, hunting is real,
It's nature.

Jedd Rawlings (11)
Horn Park Primary School, Lee

Untitled

My bushy tail turns to rust,
I gave them all I could
In trust.
I travel around on my own,
Next thing you know,
You will see my bones.
I cannot control my mood,
It's not my fault,
I have no food.

Ahmet Akis
Horn Park Primary School, Lee

Dancing Bear

Heartsick creature dancing scared
Emotionless eyes blinking everywhere
Controlled by a human with no brain
Big chains held him down while he howled in pain
Once was proud and magnificent
But now bruised, battered and bent
The fate of the bear:
Man-made.

Alfie Hadley (10) & Steven Hayes (11)
Horn Park Primary School, Lee

A Pro Footballer

Football's fun, football's sad,
Sometimes we get mad.
But look, in the end it brings the world together.
I have trained my mind
And now my body will follow.
Who am I? I am the champion.
In the field of dreams you will never walk alone.
Football!

Mohammed Sajid Hoque (8)
Lawdale Junior School, Bethnal Green

Dear Mother

You are the reason I'm here,
I love you more than a flower needs water.
I know sometimes I don't show you how much I love you,
But I let you know this,
I love you and I will love you till the day I die.
I love you.
The meaning of mum:

M arvellous
U nderstanding
M otherly!

Sumayya Hoque (10)
Lawdale Junior School, Bethnal Green

The Passions Of My Life

The summer breeze,
The gentle sway of trees,
As I sing my song,
Of sweet sounds short and long,
This is what I find nice,
The passions of my life . . .

The winter snow,
Look at it go!
As I write my story,
As big as a lorry,
This is what I find nice,
The passions of my life.

The autumn leaves,
Falling from the trees,
As I plant my seeds,
I'll see to their needs,
This is what I find nice,
The passions of my life.

The spring flowers blossom,
My brother will toss 'em,
The birds singing tunefully,
As I play happily.
This is what I find nice,
The passions of my life.

Today we celebrate,
Eid, Christmas, New Year,
The day will decide our fate,
We will remember this date,
This is what I find nice,
The passions of my life.

Naznina Begum (10)
Lawdale Junior School, Bethnal Green

Weird Seasons

Spring is warm,
Food finally growing in a farm,
People won't harm,
Dirty palms,
Crazy animals need to be calm,
Lovely curry like dahl,
Fun games played with a ball.

Summer is hot,
Fry an egg in a pot,
Babies sleep in a cot,
Sentences end with a dot,
Maths has loads of jots,
Pies to eat a lot,
Food goes rot.

Autumn is cool,
Bad boys are a fool,
Swimming in a pool,
Sleeping in a soft wool,
Fix cars with tools,
Horses don't rule,
Wake early just to go to school.

Winter is cold,
In snow hard to hold,
Hands stiff to fold,
Difficult to find gold,
Everything is sad,
Secrets have been told,
People can't write bold.

Sabrina Akthar (9)
Lawdale Junior School, Bethnal Green

Victoria, Victoria

Victoria, Victoria,
With her smooth, black hair,
And her face white and fair.
The prince's black bow ties,
The princess' golden eyes.
They both get ready for the ballroom in town,
With the princess' golden gown.
And the prince's black shirt
Without a slight bit of dirt.
They danced and twirled,
They spun and curled
Under the ballroom and the gallery,
By the garden wall and balcony,
A gleaming shape she floated by,
Between the tall houses high.
The sound of a gunshot,
The princess was caught!

Who is this and what is here?
And the lighted palace near?
Died the sound of a royal cheer,
And they crossed themselves for fear.
The prince said, 'She had a lovely face,
God in His mercy lend her grace!'
She died there on the bed,
Cold and dead!

Cyma Aktar (11)
Lawdale Junior School, Bethnal Green

The Weather

The wind shouted out with rage,
Roaring fiercely, turning a page.
Its face was as dark as the darkness,
Creeping over the moon's bright face,
Its feet were stomping up and down loudly
As if it were in a race.
The rain poured down very, very heavily,
It was so loud,
Everyone could hear it in Beverley.
The sun gleamed as bright as a golden coin resting,
Its pretty eyes were peering down
On some birds nesting.
It was so sunny,
While everyone was selling money.
Suddenly, the grey cloud started to cry,
Covering everything, leaving nothing dry.
It began to rain and rain,
You couldn't see Brick Lane.
But when it became night,
Everybody slept tight.

Moumi Qurayshi (9)
Lawdale Junior School, Bethnal Green

My Cat

My wonderful cat,
Sits on a stiff mat,
All day long,
So that's why he smells wrong!

He wears a strange hat,
In the shape of a rat,
On his furry head,
Which is really, really red.

I like my cat,
But he's really fat.
I'm glad I own him
And not next-door's Tim!

Masuma Rahman (11)
Lawdale Junior School, Bethnal Green

The Beach

As the shimmering, bright, flaming sun,
Shone above the white, fluffy clouds,
On the snow-cleared sky full of clouds
As if it was drifting to sleep.
Above the bright turquoise, crystal sea,
The waves washing against the shore.

Crabs as diminutive as baby turtles,
Crawled the deserted beach at noon,
The soft, powdery sand crunching
As baby turtles crawling to the glimmering sea.

As the golden, glossy stars twinkled above,
The silver, sparkly moonlight,
On the dark, dull sky.
The mother turtles laid their eggs
And left them there under the dark, dull sky.

As the dark sky's breeze twirled
Around the deserted beach
One could hear the sound of cracking!

Jannah Yeasmin (11)
Lawdale Junior School, Bethnal Green

The Young Deer

When I'm quiet, very quiet, I can hear . . .
Galloping horses in the swaying of the calm meadow,
Freezing like ice in the Arctic when is in danger's way,
Beautiful as butterflies on a creaky branch,
The young deer learning how and what to say.

When I'm quiet, very quiet, I can hear . . .
Mothers approaching her silently while looking for danger,
Rapid gunshots in every direction,
The deer settling down in the rustling leaves
Like a sleepy workman.

When I'm quiet, very quiet, I can hear . . .
Birds chirping as she wakes in the early morning dawn,
Clattering throughout the bright, sunny forest,
Wise fathers in the lush, green hills of the buzzing meadow.

Hajara Jarrin (10)
Lawdale Junior School, Bethnal Green

Dream A While With Me

I dream of rainbows, bright in the sky,
I dream of lightning, together we cry.

I dream of flowers, I feel such delight,
I dream of spiders and I scream with fright!

I dream of fish, swimming in the sea,
I dream of sharks, coming after me!

I dream of lambs, walking around,
I dream of wolves, hunting with no sound.

I dream of children, several of them ours,
I dream of them shouting, being up for hours.

Stay with me forever and together we'll cope,
Because when I dream of you, I dream of hope.

Dream awhile with me and together we'll see,
Not all dreams are bad, so dream along with me!

Anisah Begum Ali (11)
Lawdale Junior School, Bethnal Green

In My Sandwich

In my sandwich there's:
Pickles and tickles,
Pears and dares,
Sugarcanes and big brains,
Kidneys and bees,
Milk and a bunch of silk,
The inside of a goat and an ancient boat
And still more and more.

In my sandwich there's:
Peas and trees,
Toffee and the North Sea,
Lollipops and fancy tops,
Pancakes and poisoning snakes,
Jelly beans and mini teens,
By eating my sandwich,
I wonder if I can eat more.

Radia Aktar (10)
Lawdale Junior School, Bethnal Green

My Funny, Wonderful Family

My mum works, cooks
She loves sleeping
And is always reading books!

My dad loves to work and eat
Even though he is busy
For me he does his bit.

My brother really knows how to annoy
Also constant teasing and always on the phone
And I really wish he would sometimes go away
And then tells that I moan!

Me, I like being honest,
In life I want to achieve the best
By aiming high
I will find life's treasure chest.

Inayah Naima (9)
Lawdale Junior School, Bethnal Green

What Is . . . The Sun?

The scorching sun is a huge blazing furnace,
The glittering sun is a golden coin zoomed into the max,
It is a blistering fireball with licking flames,
And a mammoth dazzling light bulb hanging in the turquoise sky.
It is a twinkling, golden dinghy sailing on the blue curtain,
A bunch of bursting flames forming a circle in the sky,
It is a table lamp beaming across the ocean-blue wallpaper,
It is an orange, roaring inferno exploding in the blue sky.
The golden sun is a shimmering beach ball blazing in the sky,
It is a giant's thumbprint exploring the blue paper.
The sun is a gigantic torch sharing decent light,
The sun is a huge radiator providing us free heat.

Mohammed Rabbi (11)
Lawdale Junior School, Bethnal Green

Weather

Weather, weather, in the sky,
When it's bright the birds will fly.

In spring the flowers grow,
And the farmers have lots of crows.

When it's breezy the leaves will fall,
In some places not at all.

In summer, no more school,
It's so hot, we go to the pool.

In winter, snow will drop,
Make sure you wear comfy tops.

Taklima Yesmin (9)
Lawdale Junior School, Bethnal Green

Channel!

Acceptance of darkness, the heart of sun,
The battle is over, the people have won!

Ether of sunlight, dust of stars,
Eyes against nothing, know nothing is far.

Blue opalescence that holds in the night,
Vanish forever, in infinite light.

Eyes of the humans, hand of the sun,
The old life is over, the new life has begun!

Tasnia Aktar (11)
Lawdale Junior School, Bethnal Green

People

Busy businessmen bribe with beer,
Funny football fans laugh with cheer.

Panicking policemen parp all day,
Terrible teachers hardly pay.

Dreadful doctors give prescriptions,
Petrified pupils give descriptions.

Brainy barristers babble in court,
Terrible teenagers always talk.

Fariha Ishrat (9)
Lawdale Junior School, Bethnal Green

Is This The End?

Shining stars right above me
I can't see the stars any more
My heart is breaking apart
Tyre wheels squeaking like a squirrel
Revenge is not in my heart any more
Beans that look like vomit
Fat fish all over me
What is love?
Towering banana peels all over me
Singing?
Just like tap dancing
I wonder what Nellie is doing?
Darkness is falling over me
Is this the end of my life?

Nikita Mwanza (8)
Redriff Primary School, Rotherhithe

Untitled

Rivers glow like gold
Glittering like fireworks
The sun is baking.

Archie Mehmet (9)
Redriff Primary School, Rotherhithe

I Feel Lonely

Twinkly, glittery, shining stars sparkle upon me
Too much darkness
Now completely dark
The darkness shades over me
My heart pounding faster
Rubbish building up on top of me
I miss the peace, love and comfort
I miss Nellie
I feel lonely
Fleshy fillets and bony fish clog my nose
Wind blowing like crystal clear white birds flying in the sky
The breeze blowing my dress
My heart racing.

Suad Jones (8)
Redriff Primary School, Rotherhithe

So Lonely

I want my old life back
The sight of the stars glimmering directly towards me
Someone singing as loud as cars crashing into one another
What is this? Bright banana peels pile on my face
Revolting, rotten rubbish towering and towering over me
Expired bread that could have been fed to the ducks,
Now the stars don't glow, only pitch-black and darkness!
Wet Coke fizzing on my toes
Is that a dog barking?
Woof! Woof!
Lying lifeless
Love is spreading all over me
So lonely.

Kiara Rowe (7)
Redriff Primary School, Rotherhithe

Where Is Love?

I can hear a tyre squeaking like a hungry squirrel wanting a nut
Loud, awful singing
Is it water dripping?
Rubbish, I smell like I didn't wash
As the night goes by I wish I was by a fireplace
But I'm not
I'm in the freezing cold
A soggy, disgusting dribble drips down my face like I'm sweating
One minute anger, the other minute revenge
No more twinkling, glimmering stars shine upon me
Do I hear barking?

Where is love?

Gracie Hicks (7)
Redriff Primary School, Rotherhithe

Is It Love?

Mouldy bacon falling on top of me as each day goes past
My scent is of old orange peels becoming stronger every day
I see nothing but darkness
I wonder what I feel rubbing against me?
I wonder what's blowing against me in the night?
But it's only tyres with holes in
Thrown in the dump every day and night
I'm scared when I hear them they give me a fright
Every night I feel something in my heart
I think to myself
Is this love?

Molly Easter (8)
Redriff Primary School, Rotherhithe

River - Haiku

Crystal clear water.
My life is just beginning.
Bubbling down mountains.

Denise Nantongo (9)
Redriff Primary School, Rotherhithe

Is This A Dream?

Twinkling, glittery stars shine like a shiny rainbow.
I feel lonely.
Crunchy cans
Stinking strawberry
Is this a dog barking?
Is my heart saying it wants to go to Nellie and Lawrence
Or is it saying it wants to go to Abilene and Palligrena?
Am I seeing a dream?
Or is this going to happen in the future?
Or is this happening for real?

Aparajita Sandhu (8)
Redriff Primary School, Rotherhithe

Is This The End Of Me?

Dark, dirty rubbish in front of me
A pain in my chest
Thinking of Abilene, Nellie and Lawrence
Do they miss me?

I'm sure someone will come and get me soon
I can feel my heart beating in and out
Abilene loved me
What have I done?

Is this the end of me?

Lily-Rose Payne (7)
Redriff Primary School, Rotherhithe

At The Dump

Darkness is falling over me,
Where is my family?
I can feel banana peels,
Mouldy mangos next to me,
Too much darkness, I cannot see,
Love is tearing through my heart,
The smell of smoke zooming up my nose,
Mind-blowing noises.

Finn Lawless (7)
Redriff Primary School, Rotherhithe

Could This Be The End?

Could this be the end?
Am I going to die?
Help me
Where are you, nice Nelly?
I am as sad as a lonely dog
I am scared
Is it love I smell?
Am I in a grave?
What was that?

Carl West (8)
Redriff Primary School, Rotherhithe

Anger And Revenge

Crunching rubbish in the centre of the dump
The smell of mouldy mash
The sharp feel of squashed cans
I can see slimy goo
The smell of bubbling vinegar
The smell of burnt toast
I feel revenge in my heart
All I feel is darkness
Anger and revenge.

Joe Goodfield (7)
Redriff Primary School, Rotherhithe

Better Than Being At Sea

The smell of rotting rubbish moving on top of me
Can I hear a dog?
I feel so angry
Because of Lolly!
I feel so lonely here at the rubbish dump
I wish Abilene was here
I really miss her and want her to rescue me
Do I miss Nellie and Lawrence too?
At least it's better than being at sea.

Aaliyah Morris (7)
Redriff Primary School, Rotherhithe

My Heart Is Breaking

Stars shining as bright as a rainbow
My heart is going to break apart
The shining stars that I can't see any more
Why am I all alone in this dump?
My heart is breaking
What is love all about?
About to cry
Why did Lolly do this?
My dress is ripped.

Alix Mortier (7)
Redriff Primary School, Rotherhithe

My Heart Is Breaking Apart

Smelly, stinky Coke bottles next to me,
Vomit all over me, blocking my nose,
Crashing rubbish banging my head,
Clouds of dust giving me a cough,
Darkness, I miss the stars,
Lots of fish bones all over me,
My heart is breaking apart.
I feel love.

Romeo Barr (8)
Redriff Primary School, Rotherhithe

Stuck In The Rubbish

Mouldy orange peels
Rubbish that smells like rotten strawberries
Crumbs of crisps falling on me like a mountain of snow
Moulding fish squashing on me
A man singing . . .
'I am the king of the world.'
What is love?

Millie Wildego (7)
Redriff Primary School, Rotherhithe

Nightmare

Mouldy banana skins, fiddling around me
Pumping tyres creating towers
Bubbling vinegar scratching and rotting in its way
Popping bottles, flying with the wind
Enormous cranes tugging in and yanking out
Abilene, where are you?
I want you back with me.

Samuel Frederick (8)
Redriff Primary School, Rotherhithe

I Want Revenge

Why is there rubbish all over me?
Where am I?
I want revenge on Lolly!
Where are Nellie and Lawrence?
The smell of stinky, smelly rubbish on top of me.
Who is this stranger?

Sid Gilbert (7)
Redriff Primary School, Rotherhithe

River - Haiku

Gleaming in the sun
Birds leap up high in the sky
Now this is the life!

Kittie Mae Hastings (10)
Redriff Primary School, Rotherhithe

River - Haiku

Swirling down mountains,
Fish gossiped underneath me,
Life is so much fun!

Anika Vajagic (9)
Redriff Primary School, Rotherhithe

River - Haiku

They're adorable
Dance and flutter merrily
My ballerinas!

Michael Akintoye (9)
Redriff Primary School, Rotherhithe

River - Haiku

Revolting river
Dreaming about the good days
What could I have been?

Jade Olusanya (9)
Redriff Primary School, Rotherhithe

River - Haiku

It was a gone time
Time before factories grew
Brick by greedy brick . . .

Bolanle Akinkunle (9)
Redriff Primary School, Rotherhithe

River - Haiku

Then a disaster -
Monsters were built brick by brick
Will this ever stop?

Arbër Mehmeti (9)
Redriff Primary School, Rotherhithe

River - Haiku

I am not a bin
I am a splashing river
Will you ever stop?

Lauren Harper (9)
Redriff Primary School, Rotherhithe

Polluted Destruction - Haiku

Gruesome, revolting
Life lived now as dark as death
A life has been claimed.

Kate Moses (9)
Redriff Primary School, Rotherhithe

River - Haiku

Grey smoke like thunder,
Flowers gasping for fresh air,
Black smoke like a bomb.

Holly Holding (9)
Redriff Primary School, Rotherhithe

Poisoned River - Haiku

Smoke is killing me,
Clouds of poison have appeared.
Will this ever end?

Emma Elsley (9)
Redriff Primary School, Rotherhithe

Ripple Of Peace - Haiku

A ripple of peace
Metallic blue gift of life
Indisposable.

Salimah Bah (9)
Redriff Primary School, Rotherhithe

Love Birds - Haiku

Blossoms spring to life
Means one's true love is calling
Comforting, soft heart.

Lucy Holmes (9)
Redriff Primary School, Rotherhithe

Haiku

Blinded by darkness
Freedom will be endangered
Peace is imprisoned.

Yasmin Marcos (9)
Redriff Primary School, Rotherhithe

Poisoned River

Deafening sirens
Abandonment of radiance
Rivers of poison.

Jazmin Nwosu-Ekpete (10)
Redriff Primary School, Rotherhithe

Running Out Of Ideas

I have run out of ideas
But more are on their way.
Are they hiding and running from me?
I need one before everything goes wrong.

My ideas are dying out.
I need to feed them something good.
Finally, my imagination machine
Starts up and my ideas are coming back to me
Like a seed growing.

So now I'm closing down my machine but no -
'Pop' my idea came.
But it came out of my head so fast
I can't remember it.
But 'pop' it came back
So I quickly jotted it down.

Rebecca Mukasa (10)
St James Hatcham CE Primary School, New Cross

The Ideas That Always Come And Go

Have you ever had a wonderful idea that comes and goes?
Where it's gone nobody knows.
Well, that's what happens to Rose.
She wants to be a lawyer
But - as to ideas - she can't think of one.
Where has it gone?
Is it shy
Or trying to be sly?
Or what now? She wants to be an engineer
But all her ideas seem to smear.
She thinks of another idea but it is rubbish again.
When she grew up she had a wonderful idea
Of being a doctor.
Now she knows what ideas are for.

Enitoluwafe Adesile (9)
St James Hatcham CE Primary School, New Cross

Input

The ideas that run through my mind are very logical.
They are like a number machine
Where you have a rule and a number
And it goes through my mind,
Looks for a solution and results in an answer.
My mind is kind of like a computer
Because when someone types something in
And it is wrong, then it will notify you
Then correct the answer.
In another way my mind is not like a computer
Because a computer has to wait for information
To be input, but my mind has its own initiative.

Oluwaseun Akinsiwaju (11)
St James Hatcham CE Primary School, New Cross

The Idea That Got Lost For One Second

Ideas dazzling through my mind,
So hard for them to stop.
Ideas like a puppy, boasting and boasting.
My idea, like a puppy asking for help.
Suddenly I was thinking,
Then it zoomed past my mind.
I thought and thought but I still couldn't remember.
I saw a puppy and it popped into my head again.

Bayode Abass (8)
St James Hatcham CE Primary School, New Cross

My Magic Box
(Based on 'Magic Box' by Kit Wright)

I will put in the box . . .

A stickman on a motorbike,
The first season of the world,
A dragon's first fire breath.

I will put in the box . . .

The first Barcelona Premier League,
The biggest first dinosaur,
A snowball as big as a volcano.

I will put in the box . . .

A dragon with spiky hair,
The first smile of a kitten
And Kaka's first goal.

I will put in the box . . .

A cowboy in a classroom,
A donkey in a football match
And the most delicate flower.

My box is fashioned from chocolate and plastic
With footballs on the lid and diamonds.

I shall fly in my box
Through the Atlantic Ocean and
Land on a tropical island.

Bachir Moujahid (8)
St Luke's CE Primary School, Islington

The Magic Box
(Based on 'Magic Box' by Kit Wright)

I will put in the box . . .

Shooting stars on Bonfire Night,
A hairy monster in its underwear
With a walking stick,
A shark that's dancing around the sea.

I will put in the box . . .

A first snowflake in the summer,
A first bloom of a golden flower in the spring,
Finding the end of a rainbow.

I will put in the box . . .

Haley's comet passing by
To wait for another 76 years,
A spike from a Christmas tree covered with snow
And the galaxy coming to Earth.

I will put in the box . . .

The king eating the first ripe fruit in a garden,
A first car
And a willow tree,
Hair blowing and granting wishes.

My box is fashioned from gold and sparkles,
With the United Kingdom flag on the lid
And its corners with glitter on them.
Its hinges are chocolate bars
And its front is colourful as the rainbow.

I shall fly on my box
Through the candyfloss clouds,
Then land on the highest building in New York
And look at all the people in Times Square.

Kimberly Onen (9)
St Luke's CE Primary School, Islington

The Magic Box
(Based on 'Magic Box' by Kit Wright)

I will put in my box . . .

A grandma doing graffiti on the wall,
Harry Potter on the flying horse,
Ellis dancing with the ruler.

I will put in my box . . .

A footballer turning into a teacher in two seconds,
A LEGO tower that never gets knocked down,
Glasses dancing to the radio.

I will put in my box . . .

The first band to be made
And get booed off the stage,
Christmas in summer,
A rainbow having a food fight.

I will put in my box . . .

The lick of the loveliest lolly,
The first step of a child
And a baby walking for the first time.

My box is fashioned from dragon's fire
And the silver look of the disco ball,
With a colourful rainbow on the lid
And a chocolate bar in the corner.
Its hinges are covered with the smell of perfume
And the images of bright stars.

I shall ride in my box (rocket)
At the speed of a race car,
Across . . .
Then land on a street full of adventures.

David Tabala (8)
St Luke's CE Primary School, Islington

The Magic Box
(Based on 'Magic Box' by Kit Wright)

I will put in the box . . .

A chocolate bar running away from you,
The love of a family,
An elf with a pet hamster.

I will put in the box . . .

Toys as big as humans,
Someone getting married,
Wires made out of mud.

I will put in the box . . .

Bread toasting itself,
Christmas every week,
Going to the pantomime every day.

I will put in my box . . .

December in summer,
Baby's first birthday
And snow in June.

My box is fashioned from gold, sparkly love,
Hearts and curly white hair,
With jewels in the corners.
Its hinges are made out of bendy chocolate bars.

I shall ride my box
Down a big snowy hill,
Then land in Lapland
With children making snow angels
On the white blanket.

Ronni-Rose Rowland (8)
St Luke's CE Primary School, Islington

All About Me

A rtistic Amie also sings
M arvellously funny and always moves
I nterestingly fun but really silly
E nergetic and dances all the time.

Amie O'Connor (9)
St Luke's CE Primary School, Islington

The Magic Box
(Based on 'Magic Box' by Kit Wright)

I will put in my box . . .

The first building in Earth's age,
A chocolate bar that never melts
And the first gold from a rainbow.

I will put in my box . . .

Coffee that never runs out,
A clock that can take you to the future,
A key that can open any door.

I will put in my box . . .

One drop from the Red Sea,
The Doctor's screwdriver
And a pet hamster that can transform into a bird.

I will put in my box . . .

A piece of paper that cannot tear,
A bug that is the size of London
And a telescope that can go far out.

My box is made from
Lava from Mount Etna
With shooting stars on the lid
And keys in the corners.
Its hinges are made from dragon teeth.

I shall fly in my box
In a cloud of rain,
Passing the Statue of Liberty,
Then land on the steam of Mount Etna.

Joshua Guy (9)
St Luke's CE Primary School, Islington

Seasons

Spring:
Spring is growth,
Where flowers and fruits grow.
Spring is in the air.
Stems that are green.
Spring is the time for children to have fun.

Summer:
It's fresh morning sun.
Summer is here.
Children are happy.
It's the time to have some fun.
It's hot and breezy,
That is summer.

Autumn:
Autumn is the time
When red, golden green and yellow leaves
Fall off the trees.
It is windy and cold.
There's not much to do
In autumn.

Winter:
Winter is cold, frosty with snow.
Snowflakes fall on the ground.
Get your hats, gloves and scarves.
Go outside and have fun
Building snowmen in the snow.
How much fun it is in the snow.

These are all the seasons.

Fatjona Palushi (10)
St Luke's CE Primary School, Islington

The Magic Box
(Based on 'Magic Box' by Kit Wright)

I will put in the box . . .

A lick of the loveliest lolly,
A LEGO tower that never gets knocked down,
A rainbow having a food fight.

I will put in the box . . .

The first smile of a baby,
Christmas in summer,
Horrid Henry popping out of the TV screen.

I will put in the box . . .

A child's first book of jokes,
A flower's first petal
And a pair of glasses dancing to the radio.

I will put in the box . . .

A chunk of the oldest fossil,
Harry Potter flying on a flying horse
And treasure from the secret mine.

My box is fashioned from dinosaur skin on the lid,
With gold from the magic cave
And hinges made from dragons' claws.
There are fossil pieces in the corners.

I shall surf in my box
On the deep sea of the wild Atlantic,
Then end up in the shallow sea near the seaside
As calm as a fish in its tank.

Ellis Harris (9)
St Luke's CE Primary School, Islington

Robbery

When there was a robbery, everyone ran and cried.
The police siren went screaming loud.
I went mad because I heard the investigation was going bad.
Maybe it will stop or maybe not!
Help me, Dad!

Islam Muhammed Kadri (10)
St Luke's CE Primary School, Islington

The Magic Box
(Based on 'Magic Box' by Kit Wright)

I will put in the box . . .

A first spark of a Chinese dragon at New Year,
A king eating ripe fruit,
A monster in his underwear.

I will put in the box . . .

A shark dancing around the sea,
The first bloom of a golden flower,
Shooting stars on Bonfire Night.

I will put in the box . . .

A first car in 1977,
A willow tree which is hairy,
A boy getting his medal.

I will put in the box . . .

A galaxy coming down to Earth,
A first rock that was found,
A chocolate bar which is everlasting.

My box is fashioned from crystals,
LEGO and tortoiseshell on the lid
And facts in the corner,
Its hinges are made from cheetahs' teeth.

I shall surf in my box
On the great ocean of wild Atlantic,
Then land on the bright shore
The colour of the sun.

Mustafa Kidher (8)
St Luke's CE Primary School, Islington

The Magic Box
(Based on 'Magic Box' by Kit Wright)

I will put in the box . . .

The first scent of a flower,
A clown with a long, squeaky nose,
A unicorn dressed as a dog.

I will put in the box . . .

The first person to ever be created,
The first song sung by a blackbird,
The first day of summer.

I will put in the box . . .

The first pyramid in Egypt,
Sandwiches made from sand and witches
And the first blossom of a flower.

I will put in the box . . .

The first steps of a baby,
The love of a family
And the last person ever alive.

My box is fashioned from snow and ice,
With red tortoise legs and a gold lock.
Its hinges are shiny crystals.

I shall fly in my box,
Through the high sky, passing through the clouds,
Then get portalled to a space station
Through a black hole as large as the sun.

George Petters (8)
St Luke's CE Primary School, Islington

The Snowstorm

The snow fell like a bird flying in the wind
When it fell on your head it felt fluffy and warm
It was like a Christmas card scene
You could slip over white ice
I just have to get home for my hot milk
And get out of this cold, cold, cold storm.

Jacob Donaldson (9)
St Luke's CE Primary School, Islington

The Magic Box
(Based on 'Magic Box' by Kit Wright)

I will put in the box . . .

The love of a family,
A mother watching her child grow up,
Stars coming in the sunlight.

I will put in the box . . .

The galaxy coming to Earth,
A grumpy leprechaun,
The touch of a kitten.

I will put in the box . . .

The Milky Way coming to Earth,
A war against flowers and bees
And a tree full of gummy bears.

I will put in the box . . .

The biggest dinosaur,
A shower of money
And aliens bringing peace to Earth.

My box is fashioned from a mosaic of crystal pearls,
With works of art on the sides.
Its hinges are diamonds,
The lock and the corners are made of gems.

I shall walk through the Pacific Ocean
On a dinosaur fossil,
Then wash a tree the colour of rubies.

Sakina Buhari (8)
St Luke's CE Primary School, Islington

Boys!

Boys are cool, as cool as an ice cube.
Also as sharp as a razor.
Boys are the best and my best.
Boys rule better than a king.
Boys are good at everything.
Boys are so cool, they make girls drool.

Micah Agyen (10)
St Luke's CE Primary School, Islington

The Magic Box
(Based on 'Magic Box' by Kit Wright)

I will put in my box . . .
A first ever taste of a marshmallow,
The first sneeze in a tissue,
A 13th month.

I will put in my box . . .
The first channel on a Sky box,
The best computer on Earth,
Caramel chocolate medicine.

I will put in my box . . .
Money growing on a tree,
A first ever egg from a chicken
And a kangaroo with a 3rd leg.

I will put in my box . . .
The first snow dropping from the sky,
The biggest building on the planet
And Christmas in July.

My box is fashioned from glass, gold and concrete
With tennis balls on the lid and dog paws as the hinges,
A sword as the key and two wings on the side.

I shall surf in my box
Through the skies of London
To Buckingham Palace where I will have hot chocolate
With the Queen.

Jay Gallacher (9)
St Luke's CE Primary School, Islington

The Magic Box
(Based on 'Magic Box' by Kit Wright)

I will put in the box . . .

An athlete winning his first medal,
A man in a chicken suit,
A rocket blasting off to space.

I will put in the box . . .

A child getting his first Christmas gift,
A boxer smelling his flower garden,
A pair of pants hiding in the wardrobe.

I will put in the box . . .

A hairy pig with an appetite for lettuce,
A leprechaun's share of gold
And an elephant on a unicycle.

I will put in the box . . .

A comic that goes on forever,
A mouse the size of an elephant
And three gold eggs from Greggs.

My box is fashioned from titanium and gold
With smiles on the lid
And satellites in the corners.

I shall skate in my box
Over ramps so high
You can't see them
Then ride over to the cinema.

Olamide Johnson (8)
St Luke's CE Primary School, Islington

The Magic Box
(Based on 'Magic Box' by Kit Wright)

I will put in the box . . .

The first taste of a marshmallow,
A thirteenth month,
The first people on Earth.

I will put in the box . . .

Christmas in July,
A car with a fifth wheel,
The first snow dropping from the sky.

I will put in the box . . .

A talking bookshelf,
Winter in June,
And the tallest building.

I will put in the box . . .

Some caramel medicines,
Raining money,
And the best computer.

My box is fashioned from
Ice rabbit fur and golden flowers
With marshmallows in the corners
And crystals on the lid.

I shall fly in my box,
Passing the golden rainbow.
I will land in Transylvania, the colour of a dragon.

Diana Curejova (9)
St Luke's CE Primary School, Islington

The Magic Box
(Based on 'Magic Box' by Kit Wright)

I will put in the box . . .

Toys as big as humans,
Wires made out of mud
And a baby's first birthday.

I will put in the box . . .

An elf with a pet hamster,
Chocolate running away,
The love of a family.

I will put in the box . . .

Summer in December,
Someone getting married,
Snow in June.

I will put in the box . . .

Bread toasting itself,
Christmas every day
And a baby's first word.

My box is fashioned from
Dragon skin with magic doors on the lid,
And gold secrets in the corners.
Its hinges are dragon teeth.

I shall fly in my box
Across the great Atlantic,
Then land in the North Pole.

Fahim Muhammad Miha (8)
St Luke's CE Primary School, Islington

The Magic Box
(Based on 'Magic Box' by Kit Wright)

I will put in my box . . .

Shooting stars on Bonfire Night,
A boy winning his first trophy,
The first fossil that was found.

I will put in my box . . .

A shark that's dancing around in the sea,
A willow tree with its hair blowing and making a wish,
A walking shadow cat jumping everywhere.

I will put in my box . . .

A chocolate bar going to a bar and walking to a sweet shop,
The galaxy coming to Earth,
The first day of summer.

I will put in my box . . .

A hairy monster from an underwater sea,
A first blossom of a golden flower
And the first car.

My box is fashioned from fire and ice,
With icicles on the handle.
The hinges are made from chocolate bars.

I shall surf on my box,
Over the great white sea of the Pacific Ocean.
I will land on a hot lava volcano
And look at the view.

Kyron Wong (8)
St Luke's CE Primary School, Islington

The Magic Box
(Based on 'Magic Box' by Kit Wright)

I will put in the box . . .

A talking football,
The first cub of a baby panda,
Going time travelling with The Doctor from Doctor Who.

I will put in the box . . .

A first step of a baby,
The first day of LSO,
A tiger that talks.

I will put in the box . . .

The first smell of a flower
And a first taste of a marshmallow,
The first song of a gummy bear.

I will put in the box . . .

A first child that can write his name,
A first step when a baby can walk
And a first song of a baby.

My box is fashioned from lava and gold,
With diamonds on the lid and wings in the corners,
Its bottom has the claws of a fearsome dragon.

I shall fly in my box
In the great high sky,
Going through the fluffy clouds,
Then land on the top of the Great Wall of China.

Edvin Cai (9)
St Luke's CE Primary School, Islington

The Magic Box
(Based on 'Magic Box' by Kit Wright)

I will put in the box . . .

An athlete winning his first medal
A rocket blasting to space
A man in a chicken suit

I will put in the box . . .

A leprechaun's share of gold
A child getting his first Christmas gift
An elephant on a unicycle

I will put in the box . . .

An Olympics where children can enter
A pair of pants hiding in the wardrobe
And a tree that grows money on it

I will put in the box . . .

A hairy pig with an appetite for lettuce
A leprechaun who has a pet hamster
And three gold eggs from a golden chicken

My box is fashioned from gold and silver
With satellites in the corners
Its hinges are bendy carnivores

I shall fly on my box
Through the soft cloud and gushing wind
Then land on top of the Eiffel Tower
And look at the sunrise.

Rajon Deb (9)
St Luke's CE Primary School, Islington

The Magic Box
(Based on 'Magic Box' by Kit Wright)

I will put in the box . . .

The first blossom of a flower,
The first song sung by a blackbird,
A unicorn dressed as a dog.

I will put in the box . . .

The first pyramid in Egypt,
The first day of summer,
A clown with a long, squeaky nose.

I will put in the box . . .

A sandwich made out of sand and witches,
The first person ever to be created
And the first scent of a flower.

I will put in the box . . .

The first cry of a baby,
A book with a never-ending story
And the first day of school.

My box is fashioned from diamonds and fur,
With wings on the side and monsters' feet in the front.
Its hinges are red crabs.

I shall surf in my box
In the highest sky through the white clouds,
Then land in a bunch of trees
And end up in Transylvania.

Rebecca Matthews (9)
St Luke's CE Primary School, Islington

The Magic Box
(Based on 'Magic Box' by Kit Wright)

I will put in the box . . .

Going time travelling with the doctor from Doctor Who
The first cub of a baby panda.
The first words of a baby.

I will put in the box . . .

The first taste of a marshmallow,
A book that talks.

I will put in the box . . .

The first smell of a flower,
A book that makes things real
And the first day of samba band.

I will put in the box . . .

The first baby that can talk,
A tiger that talks
And the first taste of a lollipop.

My box is fashioned from ice and silver,
With love hearts on the lid
And lines in the corners.
Its hinges are diamonds.

I shall fly on my box,
Through the fluffy clouds of the high sky,
Then be blown to a mysterious desert island
And explore.

Emmanuella Ankrah (8)
St Luke's CE Primary School, Islington

The Magic Box
(Based on 'Magic Box' by Kit Wright)

I will put in the box . . .

The first snow from the sky,
A 13th month,
The first people on Earth.

I will put in the box . . .

A caramel chocolate medicine,
The tallest building on Earth,
A car with a 5th wheel.

I will put in the box . . .

The first taste of a marshmallow,
The best computer on Earth
And a phone answering itself.

I will put in the box . . .

Money growing on a tree,
Finding the end of a rainbow
And shooting stars on Bonfire Night.

My box is fashioned from gold and silver,
With nails in the lid and white cat fur in the corners.
Its hinges are chicken legs.

I shall surf on my box on the River Thames
And then fly through the sky
And arrive at a huge house
With an enormous yellow beach.

Chloe Lewis (9)
St Luke's CE Primary School, Islington

The Magic Box
(Based on 'Magic Box' by Kit Wright)

I will put in the box . . .

A first scent of a blossom,
Summer in December
And an elf with a pet hamster.

I will put in the box . . .

The first snowflake in summer,
Mud wires
And an ostrich with gold braces.

I will put in the box . . .

Glasses dancing to the radio,
A dinosaur that can't find its way home
And the first hair of Louis Walsh.

I will put in the box . . .

A telly that got up and danced away
And a love of a family.

My box is fashioned from gold, silver,
Titanium and rubber
With dragon scales in the corners
And its hinges are made from dragon toenails.

I shall jet in my box
To the snowiest place on Earth
With a blanket of snow.

Muhammad Buhari (8)
St Luke's CE Primary School, Islington

Football

I'm a football, I'm very cool,
It's like basketball,
What should I do if they keep bouncing me?
I bounce, I get kicked and I spin,
Sometimes people rip me out.
What should I do?
I don't like being a football!

Imran Islam (9)
St Luke's CE Primary School, Islington

The Magic Box
(Based on 'Magic Box' by Kit Wright)

I will put in the box . . .

The first shooting star,
The first raindrop
And the first footsteps of a baby.

I will put in the box . . .

The first leaf on a tree,
The first part of nature,
The last dinosaur.

I will put in the box . . .

The light of broad daylight,
The light of the moon,
The eyeball of a dragon.

I will put in the box . . .

The spark of a flame,
The dance of the foxtrot,
The feather of a seagull.

My box is fashioned with jewels,
Gold and silver,
With jewel-encrusted hinges.

I shall fly in my box
And land on top of a tall mountain
And gaze down at the view.

Lewis Slater Horgan (8)
St Luke's CE Primary School, Islington

The Magic Box
(Based on 'Magic Box' by Kit Wright)

I will put in the box . . .

The first smile of a kitten,
The brightest star,
The first smile of a baby.

I will put in the box . . .

The first shooting star,
The first singing song.

I will put in the box . . .

Three wishes from a star,
The sip of hot chocolate
And the first born baby.

I will put in the box . . .

Five pencils pinned in a tennis ball,
A soft toy with fifteen buttons
And a button in honey.

My box is fashioned from angel wings and stars
With a flower on the side
And crystals on the corners.

I shall fly in my box
On the great fluffy clouds through the air
And land up in a fairy land.

Jackie Opuku Appiah (9)
St Luke's CE Primary School, Islington

The Tiger

His stripes are gold and yellow
Triple coloured with orange, white and black
Goes in packs for food
He runs as fast as the wind
He is the lord of the jungle
Endangered he is
Important he is
I feel he must live for our sake.

Ayman Chehab (9)
St Luke's CE Primary School, Islington

My Magic Box
(Based on 'Magic Box' by Kit Wright)

I will put in my box . . .

A robot made of sweets,
The first kiss of a unicorn,
A song of a gummy bear.

I will put in my box . . .

The first blossom of a flower,
A unicorn and a dragon with magical powers,
The Minotaur from the legend's words,
Marshmallows.

I will put in my box . . .

The freshest cup from a china shop,
The scent of a fresh waterfall
And a chocolate statue of me.

My box is fashioned from gold and steel
With hearts and stars on the lid
And gems, rubies, diamonds and crystals
All over the box.
Its hinges are snowflakes on black card.

I shall go to my world,
Meet all my friends
And drive my 'SSC Ultimate Aero II'.

Kane Melton (9)
St Luke's CE Primary School, Islington

Volcanoes

The hot, red lava of the volcano.
The steam is grey and white.
The bright red lava came out with a huge eruption.
The air is thick with choking fumes.
The haze of the smoke is unstoppable,
Like a giant, even though it isn't a giant.
The sticky lava did not stop,
No one could see each other,
The flooded sky of ash.

Dennis Dincer (10)
St Luke's CE Primary School, Islington

The Magic Box
(Based on 'Magic Box' by Kit Wright)

I will put in the box . . .

The first star in the sky,
Three-eyed monsters in a dustbin,
A magical snowman wearing clothes.

I will put in the box . . .

A treasure chest filled with socks,
The first rainforest in the Atlantic,
The first Premier League.

I will put in the box . . .

A big ice cream ruling Earth,
Dino bones muddled up with dragon bones
And Lionel Messi's first goal.

I will put in the box . . .

A dinosaur band,
The Milky Way made of milk
And a giant Oompah Loompah.

My box is fashioned from gold and titanium
With dragon wings and legs.

I shall fly in my box through the clouds
And land in Disneyland.

Shihab Hussain (8)
St Luke's CE Primary School, Islington

Music

People love music everywhere
It makes them smile and care
It makes them laugh
It makes them cry
It makes them feel alive
It's very emotional
It's very cool
It makes you want to dance!
Music is my name!

Sara Tabala (10)
St Luke's CE Primary School, Islington

My Day

I woke up this morning
As always, yawning.
My mum woke up,
I said, 'Morning.'
While the taxi was horning,
Ready to take me to school.
I put on my hood
And phoned Miss Wood,
Saying I might be late for school.
She wasn't happy at all.
I arrived at school
And went out to play only for my annoying friends
Who won't stop staying hey.
'What you been up to?' I said.
They said, 'Nothing. You?'
'Kind of. I have the fever.'
'Oh dear,' they said.
'You might have to go home
To bed.'
Then it was time to go home
To a nice hot bath full of foam.
'It's been a hard day,' I said.
I wonder what's going to happen tomorrow
And the next.

Harry Eaton (10)
St Luke's CE Primary School, Islington

Weather When We Play Out

I go out to play in the swimming pool.
When I get out I have a good wash.
I take my bike out
And ride it to my friend's house.
I go to the park every day.
It's summer.

When I wake up I see everything is wet.
I go outside and I jump in the puddles.
Everything splashes on me.
It's raining.

Rozerin Edebali (10)
St Luke's CE Primary School, Islington

The Magic Box
(Based on 'Magic Box' by Kit Wright)

I will put in the box . . .

The soft scent of my first teddy bear,
A fairy in overalls and bovver boots,
An upside-down teacher with her socks on her ears.

I will put in the box . . .

A black kitten with a pink nose,
A witch with a dog as her broomstick,
Father Christmas with his mince pie pyjamas on.

I will put in the box . . .

A game with no instructions,
The first flower in spring
And a duck wearing sunglasses.

My box is fashioned from head to toe
With leopard spots,
Chocolate in the corners
And hinges made of rabbits' teeth.
My lock is made of ice.

I shall skate in my box
To the most slippery, tallest mountains.

Mia Bassett (8)
St Luke's CE Primary School, Islington

Football

Football's fun, football's cool
It's a sport that I have to play
It's the best of all
People say football is for boys
My favourite player is Wayne Rooney
His brother's name is Layne Looney
Wayne Rooney hurt his leg because he stepped on something sharp
He stopped and sat down and he said
'If I don't play
England is going to lose.'

Riyad Kahir (10)
St Luke's CE Primary School, Islington

The Magic Box
(Based on 'Magic Box' by Kit Wright)

I will put in the box . . .

The first twinkling star,
An alien with three eyes on his feet,
The first cuddle from my mum.

I will put in the box . . .

The first sunshine,
3D shapes with cream and cherries on top,
The first love of a family.

I will put in the box . . .

The first snowflake of winter,
Hannah Montana's first song
And some bumblebee ice cream.

My box is fashioned with marble for the lock,
The Queen's gold coins for the lid
And diamonds for the hinges.

I shall surf in my box
Through sunny clouds to the highest mountain
To watch the whole world.

Chloe Zambon (9)
St Luke's CE Primary School, Islington

A Rainbow

I saw a rainbow,
It shone on me.
I went to put my sunglasses on.
I looked up.
Its massive semicircle reflected the sun.
The multicolours shone so bright.
I even know the colours off by heart.
The sky was so bright.
When the rainbow shone it made me feel relaxed.
'Come on then,' I said to my friends.
'Let's follow the rainbow to the end
And we might find a pot of gold.'

Sinead Hannon (9)
St Luke's CE Primary School, Islington

My Magic Box
(Based on 'Magic Box' by Kit Wright)

I will put in my box . . .

A pencil fighting a ruler,
Finding the end of a rainbow in the middle of a football match,
The first chocolate bar in the universe.

I will put in my box . . .

A baby lion's first smile,
A kitten's first purr,
A concert playing football.

I will put in my box . . .

A kid's first pair of cool shoes,
A football player dancing
And a kid's last joke.

My box is fashioned from metal and grass
With soft hinges and hard gold bricks in the corners.

I shall surf in my box across Islington's sunny sky
To the Arsenal stadium to play football.

James Gallacher (8)
St Luke's CE Primary School, Islington

The Night

As I walked through the night,
It was as dark as space.
The lighting flickered
As the stars formed.
It was as if they were making a picture.
Through the depths of the trees,
Owls sang tu-whit, tu-whoo.
As I walked on, wolves howled,
How they spoke.
Shadows appeared, cats miaowed.
The moon came out and said hello.
The mist swayed about waving.
Thunder banged, *boom.*
The mist cleared.

Tia Harrold (9)
St Luke's CE Primary School, Islington

My Future

I'm dreaming of my future
A loop of fantastic things
To be the best singer
To win at dance
To have the chance to fly to France
To be smiling at millions of fans as they cheer me on
When I'm singing next to my dad and Rihanna
To see my pictures in the paper and on TV
To write a stunning book
To be running to freedom with my family
Just like the birds that fly free
I want that to be me
To get married
But of course not to a man who drinks or smokes
To have two children, a girl and boy
I hope they bring me so much joy.

My name is Ruhani
And I'm looking at a bright and wonderful future!

Ruhani Nwaka Eggay Muhammad (10)
St Luke's CE Primary School, Islington

True Love

True love comes from within,
Even though it may be thin.
True love comes from within,
Life is like a dream next to him.
Long, sleepless nights,
Shy after your true love has spoken
And when you have just awoken.
Time and time again you walk into a wall
And then start to drawl.
If he is quiet,
Don't deny it,
Just live by it.
True love comes from within.

Ellie Sutherland (10)
St Luke's CE Primary School, Islington

The Magic Box
(Based on 'Magic Box' by Kit Wright)

I will put in the box . . .

The first smile of a baby lion,
Three snowmen with rumbling bellies,
The first smile of a dandelion.

I will put in the box . . .

Shooting stars on Bonfire Night,
The love of a family
And an elf with a pet hamster.

My box is fashioned from gold and steel,
With swords on the lid
And plastic sticks in the corners.

I will fly in my box
To the sunny beach of Chick Island
And then visit a pair of kings
With coconuts in their hands!

Judah Olajide (9)
St Luke's CE Primary School, Islington

My Funny Dad

My funny dad is so funny,
You'll laugh till you cry.
No one knows why he's so funny,
Some people think that his shoes
Aren't screwed on just right.
He's not very tall, but he's almost a bear.
You can tell he's old by his thick, grey hair.
My funny dad can make you laugh sometimes,
You think he's crazy, his jokes are bonkers.
Sometimes I try to make him laugh,
But it never works.
Actually, he's not just funny,
He's the funniest dad in the world.

Sam Orgill (10)
St Luke's CE Primary School, Islington

My Horse, Hazel

She rides through the wind,
She gallops through the snow,
She canters through the rain,
    My horse, Hazel.

Her eyes glitter in the sunlight,
Her hair shimmers in the moonlight,
Her fur is as brown as Belgian chocolate,
    My horse, Hazel.

Hazel is beautiful,
She's the best horse I'm ever going to get.
I love my horse, Hazel,
I'm sure she loves me back!

Madiha Islam (10)
St Luke's CE Primary School, Islington

My Name

A ctive in skipping
W aves are so beautiful
A live (fun)

C are for friends
O riginal
N ature is my thing
T rying to do my best
E motional
H appy to be at school.

Awa Conteh (9)
St Luke's CE Primary School, Islington

Butterflies

Butterflies flying all around
Happy faces in the sun
Make each other seem so young
Butterflies flapping with their wings
Happy days when they sing
Fluffy clouds all day long
Makes each other sing a song
Sitting in the garden without a fright
Listening to songs all day and night.

Emily Hold (9)
St Luke's CE Primary School, Islington

The Summer

The sun shines bright yellow, smiling from the sky
While children play in the sea
The beach is so warm
And kids eating ice cream
People sitting on the sand
Watching the massive waves
Butterflies fly in the sky
It's great fun when it's summer.

Fiona Cunningham (9)
St Luke's CE Primary School, Islington

Beach

The sun smiled upon the beach.
The sea waved and danced to the sound of tropical music.
Coconut trees jingled and jangled about.
The children screamed and played games
While the adults relaxed to the music.
The ice cream man gave out ice cream in delicious flavours.
The donkey trotted on the sand.
What fun to be on the beach!

Cheryl Gill (9)
St Luke's CE Primary School, Islington

The Sea

The sea is huge, as the waves go *splash!*
When the sun shines,
The sea makes the Earth look dull.
The sea is as blue as the sky,
The way it shines could stun my eye!
The sea is better than a pond and a river,
Once you come out of the freezing sea,
You'll begin to shiver!

Dylan Lubo (10)
St Luke's CE Primary School, Islington

Rain

Rain makes you cry
It gives you sore eyes
Rain makes you wet
And cools you in the summer
Rain makes you cover yourself
Over with an umbrella
And wish rain was never to be seen again.

Rashaan Stewart (9)
St Luke's CE Primary School, Islington

A Dragon's Tale

Once upon a time,
There lived a tropical-coloured, green-spotted dragon
Named Troop.
He was the hottest dragon.
He loved to fly and do loops.

That afternoon,
Troop was given a test to do.
It was to catch a bird and bring it back,
But he decided to bring two.

So he flew to catch his very first prey
Until he got to Swallows Cove he was thinking
What a good place to stay
And he saw a weak one so he went for the catch
But it managed to get away.

He was so depressed that he even said
'I've lost my mojo, I can't even
Catch one that is dead.'
But he saw a baby bird trying to fly
So he said to himself, 'why not try?'

But the baby bird was clever and knew he was coming
So she had an idea that involved a cave.
But the dragon was far, far away
And the baby bird said to herself, 'I am so cunning.'

Just as soon as Troop was two seconds away
The baby bird flew to the cave
But on the way he landed into a bush filled with thorns.
The dreadful dragon managed to get out
But when he did he was covered in jagged thorns
And it was hurtful when he tried to shave.

So he thought of a plan to try and get the pain away
And because he did not want the other dragons to laugh at him
He wanted to go to the kingdom so the king could get them out
So he took the hard but dangerous way.

The tropical dragon walked all the way
To the great big gates of the kingdom and was astonished
He tried to fly but he had a strong pain in his back
But he pushed the golden gates open.

He went to the king but was so ashamed to talk
The king knew what happened and what Troop wanted
So he took him out and gave him two birds
Troop flew happily and so free!

Loren Pacarada (9)
St Mary of the Angels RC School, Bayswater

I'm Afraid Of The Dark

In the night,
When it's not so bright,
The hounds bark,
I'm afraid of the dark.

Down the stairs,
I hear growling bears,
I see the haunted park,
I'm afraid of the dark.

In the backyard,
I see melted lard,
I see a strange mark,
I'm afraid of the dark.

I run to my room,
I hear a *boom!*
On the tree I see a black lark,
I'm afraid of the dark.

Abel Zemed (10)
St Mary of the Angels RC School, Bayswater

California

Ghirardelli Square

If you go to San Francisco,
While you're there
You must visit
Ghirardelli Square.

It was a chocolate factory
With a sign up in the air,
Now it is a restaurant,
But the sign's still hanging there.

You can order a chocolate mousse,
Chocolate ice cream too,
There is a chocolate-making machine
That's not at all new.

You can go to the shop
Once you finish your treat
And buy a little
Bag of sweets!

Panning for gold

If you're panning for gold
You pay five dollars
And dip your pan
In the waters.

You stand on the ground
Swish the water around
If you find some gold
Then holler!

Matteo Savant (8)
St Mary of the Angels RC School, Bayswater

My School

My school is St Mary of the Angels,
Teachers and students are like angels.
It gives me light for my future like candles,
Don't ask about homework,
There is nothing I can't handle.
I love it! I love it! I love it!

We learn at school many subjects,
Maths is easy, I play with it like objects.
Literacy is difficult, but I always do my best,
Science and history are easy, like when you rest.
I love it! I love it! I love it!

We play cricket and football,
It does not matter who scores a goal.
What matters is fun for all,
Sport is important, it helps us reach our goal.
I love it! I love it! I love it!

I hope I never leave my school
Because it is very nice and cool.
But one day we all have to go,
To do in life what you have to do.
Sadly!
I love it! I love it! I love it!

Cibelle Alves Harb (9)
St Mary of the Angels RC School, Bayswater

In The Whistling Of The Wind

In the whistling of the wind on horseback
You are striding on the back of your great chestnut,
Occasionally glancing at the other cattle rounders
And whistling the Canadian national anthem.
In the whistling of the wind you are a cruel poacher
Galloping to and fro in search of tigers,
With big cats fleeing at the fearsome sight of you.
Such is the imagination of a child that fleets
From one place to another,
Enjoying every second as if it was his last
In the whistling of the wind.

Sam Gébler (9)
St Mary of the Angels RC School, Bayswater

A School Poem

It's Wednesday morning at 6.01,
You're half asleep, your homework half done.
Your shower is cold, your Coco-Pops are dry,
Your mum forgets to kiss you goodbye.
You're walking to school, it's 7 degrees,
Your fingers won't work, your feet will freeze.
Your zipper is stuck, your right sneaker squeaks,
Your backpack straps snap, your water Thermos leaks.
You slip on the school stairs,
You trip in the hall,
The toilets flood in the bathroom stall.
The gym door is locked, library's the same,
The teacher greets you with the wrong name.
The classroom is hot, the jacket rack is packed,
Your beansprout is dead, your clay pot is cracked.
Your pencil is blunt, the sharpener jams,
Your fingers get crunched when your desktop slams.
Your maths partner's gone, your neighbour is rude,
Your teacher's again in an angry mood.
The morning bell rings, it's 8.01,
Come cosy to the whiteboard,
Another school day begun!

Michael Mendoza (8)
St Mary of the Angels RC School, Bayswater

The Sun

The sun is so bright
It's like a big light
All over the world
The sun sits and burns
And the next day
It turns to another place.

The best thing in the world
Is the sun
It's like eating a bun
That's lots of fun
There's nothing to be done
If we don't have the sun.

Roya (8)
St Mary of the Angels RC School, Bayswater

A Poem About Red

Red is an apple,
Red is a rose,
Red is the colour
Of my frozen, icy nose!

Red is my bed,
Red is my shed,
Red is the colour
Of my sewing thread!

Red is blood,
Red is a slug,
Red is the colour
Of a lady bug!

Red is lava,
Red is fire,
Red is the colour
Of people's desire!

My science book is red,
My new shoes too,
Red is my favourite colour,
What about you?

Skye Matthew-Casu (9)
St Mary of the Angels RC School, Bayswater

Football Poem

Football . . .
Football, football, football.
Some players are good and some players are bad,
But they all got a talent and that's not really sad.
There's Pele, there's Maradona and there's even more
And if you think I am lying, check on Google,
Plus a football score.
You're fast, you're slow,
But it doesn't matter because you're still on fire
And you will not blow.
You're crazy, you're mad, you will not fight,
But you will slide and tackle until your legs start to bite.

Uroliss Mendes (10)
St Mary of the Angels RC School, Bayswater

Seasons

The seasons change,
Four times a year,
From spring to winter,
They appear.

Spring is wet,
All the flowers grow,
It rains too much
And melts the snow.

Summer is hot,
It's full of shining sun,
There's no school (great!)
It's lots of fun.

Autumn is cold,
Autumn is windy,
My friend Cindy
Is practically bald.

Winter is cold,
The snowflakes fall,
We skate and ski
And make snowballs. (Woohoo!)

Fareedah Shardow (10)
St Mary of the Angels RC School, Bayswater

PE

PE, PE is fun,
Because you can play in the sun.
In PE we play cricket,
And sometimes people hit the wicket.
In PE we play football,
People foul and then they fall.
PE, PE is fun,
Because you can play in the sun.
In tennis we hit the ball over the net,
Sometimes I slip if the pitch is wet.
And we play all these things in PE,
Which makes me jolly and say *whee!*

Thiyana Nurse (10)
St Mary of the Angels RC School, Bayswater

My Friend

I have a friend
And he just lives round the bend.
Every time I go to his house
We play computer games
And he is in control of the mouse.

After that we play in the garden
Then we go to the fish and chip shop
And they give us a bargain.

Before we leave the counter
The woman shakes raindrops of vinegar
And salty snowflakes.

But when the sun goes down
And I won't tell a lie
Looks like the good days have passed me by.

One day I broke his toy
He went to tell his brother Troy
Who is eight
He kicked me out, now I don't have a mate.

Oliver Carino (9)
St Mary of the Angels RC School, Bayswater

Yellow

Yellow, yellow, like the sun
Yellow, yellow, everyone
Bright yellow from my heart
Feel the light from near and far
The seven things that we like about yellow
It's light and bright
And it's an amazing colour
It makes us laugh
It makes us smile
It beats Miley's song by a mile.

Yellow, yellow, is a butterfly flying
Flying in the sky
Yellow, yellow is a daffodil dancing
Dancing in Brazil.

Ines Guerra-Riola (10)
St Mary of the Angels RC School, Bayswater

Pizza Party

Pizza party fun at Marvy's,
Come and join the fun!
With crazy hats and flying bats,
Come on kids, let's run!

Jolly joy there's the toys,
We found them on the way,
None for you boy,
As you were hiding in the hay.

As we were done we saw Jake,
He was walking around with a gigantic cake.
He ate too much because he scoffed his face,
And ended up with a bellyache.

My friend, Taylor, needed his inhaler,
Before he could hardly breathe.
Then my friend, Leila, took him his inhaler,
And the next day he was at ease.

Michaela Da Silva (7)
St Mary of the Angels RC School, Bayswater

Santa Claus

Twinkling in the dark blue sky,
The stars shone brightly up so high.
Fluffy like feathers,
As soft as my pillow,
I sat down and ate
My scrumptious marshmallow.

Chubby, puffy, fat and dressed,
The trees sat down
To have a rest.

Ho! Ho! Ho!
Jolly, big and fat,
Who's that coming here
Wearing a big red hat?
Is it Santa Claus?
What is in his big red sack?
Presents!

Nicolle Mendoza (10) & Rayna Lavado
St Mary of the Angels RC School, Bayswater

Snow Is Falling

Snow is falling,
It delivers happiness to all.
Snow is falling,
It is better than football.

Snow is falling,
What a beautiful sight.
Snow is falling,
It sparkles in the light.

Snow is falling,
From the heavens above.
Snow is falling,
I need my hat, scarf and glove.

Snow is falling,
Let's go and play.
Snow is falling,
Let's have a fun day.

Joshua Padpu (11)
St Mary of the Angels RC School, Bayswater

My Football Poem

When I play football I always miss the goal;
My mum is even worse
She kicks it anywhere on the pitch.

When my sister watches football matches
She always roots for Spain
And when they score a goal
She falls down on the floor
And she's in pain.

When my dad plays football
He kicks it so high
And sometimes it goes
Right into the sky.
When my grandad watches the football
He shouts for Spain
And when they're winning
He eats lots of candy canes.

Luca Martinez Freitas (10)
St Mary of the Angels RC School, Bayswater

Cucumbers

Cucumbers are cool,
Cucumbers are short,
Cucumbers are soft,
But so yummy in my tummy!
Cucumbers sliced,
Cucumbers and lettuce,
Cucumbers and tomato,
But so nice in a slice of bread!
Green cucumbers,
Long and short,
Soft and tasty,
But best eaten with a cooling drink.
Salad and cucumbers,
Olive oil and vinegar,
Salt and pepper,
They all go together like the moon and the sun!

Anabela Soares (9)
St Mary of the Angels RC School, Bayswater

Cats

Cats are cute,
I had a dream that they could play the flute.
A cat would hate to wear an itchy hat.
A cat could sit all day on a comfy mat,
Some could hunt all day for a nice juicy rat.
Some cats are fat
Because all they do is sit in their owner's flat.
Naughty cats scratch the wall,
Good cats play with a bouncy ball.
When a cat is kind and sweet,
It would get a tasty treat.
When a cat is very bad,
Its owner would get very mad.
If you tease a cat, watch out,
It might get its revenge back.

Alice Lucchini
St Mary of the Angels RC School, Bayswater

Dragon Poem

One day,
In a land far away,
There lived a king named Jack
Who had a pet dragon called Mack.
Mack played with Crun,
The king's son,
But the dragon wasn't fed enough,
So he went to his friend, Cuff.
'I have nothing to eat.'
'Ah, not again, just go and beat some meat.'
So Mack went to the sea,
But all he saw was a big, blue bee.
'Yes, at last, something tasty,
I think I'm going *crazy!*'

Yassin Akhatar (10)
St Mary of the Angels RC School, Bayswater

The Mouse From New Orleans

Please give me some cheese!
I'm the mouse from New Orleans
And I dream so many dreams.

I dream of Stilton, Red Leicester and Cheddar
I've travelled the world
To find something better.

I've been to China, Japan and Australia
But I only found cheese made from Soya!

When I got to the French Rivière
I went crazy for a bite of Gruyère
And when I tasted some Parmesan
I said to this cheese, 'I'm your best fan!'

Simonpietro Magrelli (9)
St Mary of the Angels RC School, Bayswater

Steps Of Life

Life is young,
Life is 'chillaxing' in the sun,
Life is cool,
Life is school,
Life is following the rules,
Life is sad, and sometimes mad,
But having my friends
Makes my life glad,
Life gives hope, life gives love,
Life fulfils dreams well above,
As life passes and feels like all is done,
Remember to live, love, laugh
And above all, have *fun!*

Sara Lacanale (11)
St Mary of the Angels RC School, Bayswater

Was'up?

A spider crawled upon my ear
That's when I knew the true meaning of fear.
Should I call my dad
Or just scream like mad?
Spider! Oh yuck!
Is this just bad luck?
Or maybe the poor little lad
Was only feeling sad
And was looking for a hug.
So the next time you see a spider
Please don't scream in fear
It's not going to eat you up
It's just coming to say, 'Was'up?'

Brando Kennedy (10)
St Mary of the Angels RC School, Bayswater

Best Friends

I have a best friend called Bruna,
We get on so well,
We are a perfect match,
But so is sweetcorn and tuna.

Our friendship will never end,
Even if one of us had another friend.
If we ever fall out,
We will always make amends.

We've been best friends since we were four,
And every day she's knocking at my door.
We play and sing together
And pretend us best friends are on tour!

Joana Da Silva (9)
St Mary of the Angels RC School, Bayswater

Butterfly So Sweet

I am a butterfly
Flying through the air,
There's one butterfly
That's really unfair.
I drink nectar from flower to flower,
Isn't that cool?
Maybe I should go to the swimming pool!
I went to a place
That's nice and quiet today,
I made a lot of friends, hooray!

Michou Lutete (9)
St Mary of the Angels RC School, Bayswater

Mr Fly

Mr Fly flies high in the sky,
Way up high.
So Mr Fly suddenly goes down and dies
And that's the end of Mr Fly!

Oliviero Kelly (7)
St Mary of the Angels RC School, Bayswater

Jesus, My Guardian Angel

Whenever you are feeling blue,
Remember Jesus is always watching over you.
Whenever you start to fear,
Remember Jesus is always near.
Whenever you think life is tough,
Remember Jesus will help you through the rough.
Whenever you get scared at night,
Remember Jesus will be your light.
Whenever you are scared of the dark,
Remember Jesus will always keep you close to His heart.

Adam Desouza (10)
St Mary of the Angels RC School, Bayswater

Australia

A country filled with friendly smiles,
U ndersea coral that goes on for miles and miles,
S unset so bright which fills the skies,
T rees so old, full and wise,
R oos of grey, brown and red,
A land of cultures, born and bred,
L ove our food, our friends, our sports,
I sland so great that gives full support,
A ussies love life, competition as well,
    so let's bring back the Ashes and all will be swell.

Tiana Lacanale (8)
St Mary of the Angels RC School, Bayswater

The Kiwi Poem

Kiwis are sour,
Kiwis are small,
People will like them
And that's best of all.

They're always hairy,
They're also sweet,
Inside they're green,
They're lovely to eat!

Charlene Della (8)
St Mary of the Angels RC School, Bayswater

Bubblegum

Bubblegum, bubblegum, I love bubblegum,
I am addicted you see.
I enjoy it, I love it, you can't get above it.

Bubblegum, bubblegum, I love bubblegum,
My parents say if I don't stop,
I'll buy up the shop.

Bubblegum, bubblegum, I love bubblegum,
Hubba Bubba, double mint too,
Trust me, I know you'll love it too!

Flynn Ryan (9)
St Mary of the Angels RC School, Bayswater

QPR

My football team is QPR
QPR, QPR, QPR
I watch them in matches
QPR, QPR, QPR
QPR are the top of the league
QPR, QPR, QPR
My dad loves QPR
QPR, QPR, QPR
QPR are the best, forget about the rest.

Grace McKenna (10)
St Mary of the Angels RC School, Bayswater

Chips

Chips, chips
You buy them in the chip shop.

Chips, chips
Go with your fish
Go with your burger.

Chips, chips
Nanny says they're salty chips
And also tasty.

Tommaso Kelly (7)
St Mary of the Angels RC School, Bayswater

I Had A Dog Called Buster

I had a dog called Buster;
I fed him Crunchy Nut Clusters.
He loved them so much;
I thought I would add an extra touch.
In I poured honey,
He thought it was yummy.
The lot he ate whole,
Including the bowl.

Micah Ashe (11)
St Mary of the Angels RC School, Bayswater

What Am I?

I have lots of friends,
Those friends are connected to me.
I also hate fire,
If I catch on fire I will lose my friends.
I can be different colours depending on the season.
There are lots of me around the world.
It takes me ages to be big and strong.
I also help the humans to operate.
What am I?

A: A tree.

Karen Bannor (10)
St Thomas More RC Primary School, Eltham

Untitled

I am young
I am small
Everyone loves to cuddle me
I am sometimes cute
I sleep a lot
I like to hear noises
I like to chew my toys
I wake everyone up at night.
What am I?

A: A baby.

Danielle Omoregbee (10)
St Thomas More RC Primary School, Eltham

Tadpole

I am little.
When I grow up I become something green.
I am black and a bit white.
I have a little tail.
I live in the water,
But when I grow up I can jump and swim.
I have little eyes
And I have a wiggly tail!
What am I?

A: A tadpole.

Nicole Ozborne (8)
St Thomas More RC Primary School, Eltham

A Historic Poem

For nearly 1,000 years I have stood,
My wardens played host to the bad and the good.
A palace to some and a prison to others,
I've been home to kings, princesses and lovers.
A conqueror built me for London to see,
The world knows me now for my great history.

A: Tower of London.

Daniel Truss (11)
St Thomas More RC Primary School, Eltham

What Am I?

I am small,
But not very tall.
I can change colour when I touch you,
Red, purple, yellow or blue.
I have a really long tongue,
But really small lungs.
I think I'm very rare
And I don't have any hair.
What am I?

A: A chameleon.

Sharleen Nkwo (10)
St Thomas More RC Primary School, Eltham

What Am I?

I am small and pointy,
I can get rusty if you leave me in the rain.
I hold things together,
I hurt your feet if you tread on me.
I am used anywhere and everywhere,
I am just one of the millions out there.
I come in all different shapes and sizes.
What am I?

A: A nail.

Isabella Vargas (10)
St Thomas More RC Primary School, Eltham

What Am I?

I am constantly in water, but never drinking
A type of snake, but with limbs
I am slithery and slidy, unlike a snake
I never stop
Always moving
Constantly wet but always dry
What am I?

A: A shark.

Leon Mann (9)
St Thomas More RC Primary School, Eltham

What Am I?

I hop,
You can find me in a shop,
I have big ears,
Which is good for me to hear.
I come in all sizes,
I'm cuddly and cute.
What am I?

A: A rabbit.

Della Sargeant (11)
St Thomas More RC Primary School, Eltham

What Am I?

I am big.
I am extinct.
I am big.
I am brown.
I am furry.
I have big white horns.
I was alive in the Ice Age.
What am I?

Brandon-Jo Neale
St Thomas More RC Primary School, Eltham

What Am I?

If you attach me together I would be a circle.
I am shiny.
I am worn nearly everywhere.
Sometimes I'm hard to get off.
You wear me so your pants don't fall down!
What am I?

A: A belt.

Jack Sargeant (11)
St Thomas More RC Primary School, Eltham

What Am I?

I am a light in the sky.
I am like a flight in the night.
I am a flame to a fire.
I am a colourful work of art.
I am quiet but I can be loud.
I am done, now I can die.
What am I?

Emily Shorter (11)
St Thomas More RC Primary School, Eltham

A Ball

I am round and I get played with mostly every day.
People can catch me because I am sometimes light.
If you want to use me, you have to pump me up.
If you kicked me at a window, the window would smash.
If you put a hole in me, I would go down.
I come in all different colours and multicolours.
If you kick me, dogs will chase after me.

Michael Omoregbee (8)
St Thomas More RC Primary School, Eltham

What Am I?

I come in all different shapes and sizes
And all different colours.
I hold memories you can keep.
You can treasure me forever.
What am I?

A: A picture.

Molly Fitzpatrick (11)
St Thomas More RC Primary School, Eltham

Shark In The Dark

I live in the sea and glow so I can see,
When I go down deep, my glow starts to beep,
I'm some sort of shark and extremely small,
As big as 15cm - that's all!

A: A dwarf lantern shark.

Ted Hepburn (10)
St Thomas More RC Primary School, Eltham

Butterfly

I hung on a tree when I was three.
I am green now as you can see.
The birds and bees will fly with me.
Green, yellow and pink my wings will be.

Francesca Aseoche (8)
St Thomas More RC Primary School, Eltham

The Animals Of The Rainforest

Colourful parrots flying high,
Sweeping down from the sky.
Looking around for some food to eat,
Searching for that special treat.

Toucans with the big, long beaks,
Flying high above the peak.
It lives in the tall trees,
Where it can fly free.

Jaguars searching for their prey,
Sometimes it could take all day.
Oddly covered with many spots,
Often I see them with bullet shots.

Tiny tree frogs jumping from tree to tree,
Sometimes poisonous they can be.
Jumping high for all to see,
Sometimes they jump on me!

Georgia-Rose Beahan (11)
Timbercroft Primary School, Plumstead

Ten Polar Bears

10 polar bears on the ice, looking fine
One is a woman's jacket, now there are 9

9 polar bears on the ice, feeling great
One has become a rug, now there are 8

8 polar bears looking skyward to Heaven
One is a trophy, now there are 7

7 polar bears in a muddle, in a mix
One slipped in the water, now there are 6

6 polar bears too scared to dive
The polar caps are melting, now there are 5

5 polar bears clutching with their claws
Miss their mums and dads, now there are 4

4 polar bears, there were so many and now so few
2 more hunted down, now there are 2

2 polar bears on the ice, not a sound
A hunter comes along, they drag him to the ground

2 polar bears survived this year
Sadly, there's not 10 again, we shall shed a tear.

Shannon Bell (10)
Timbercroft Primary School, Plumstead

Fin Whale

I am a fin whale, this is what I must say,
I am sometimes called the greyhound of the seas.
In my pod I swim, not always freely,
When I feed I think the wild is great.
More and more of my friends going every day,
A squid came and said, 'They're coming, swim away!'

I am a fin whale, this is what I must say,
Whalers sitting on a boat looking for us.
We were struck with sadness as one of us got caught.
In my pod I swim, not always freely,
I am getting more careful every day.
We are getting more endangered every day.

Alfie Taylor (10)
Timbercroft Primary School, Plumstead

I Am A Sloth

I am a sloth eating yummy food,
I'm always in a happy mood,
I have small eyes and a smiley face,
The rainforest is my place.

My mum and dad have been taken away,
Now I sit by myself all day.
No food,
No home,
No place to stay,
When will I go?
When will be the day?

The day when I can see my dad and mum,
Then we can play and have some fun!
But then *they* come and cut down my tree,
I just want to live in harmony.

I am a sloth all alone,
Can't you see, I just want a home?

Erin Hambly (10)
Timbercroft Primary School, Plumstead

Rainforest Lay Silent

Rainforest lay silent
Where no animals are seen
Monkeys swing from tree to tree
Ants march along the forest floor
Fish swim in the river
    But . . .

Time after time tigers are dying
Skins wanted for coats
Parrots are in cages
For humans to laugh at
While mosquitoes fly about
When will someone set them free?
The rainforest is disappearing fast
Please will someone help us out?

Tariq Ameer (10)
Timbercroft Primary School, Plumstead

Life

You may think life is boring
But what you don't see
That life is quick
You have no chance to plea!

It's very extraordinary
Once chance is what you got
So make the most of it
Because some people don't have a lot.

Don't go down the wrong road
You never know when it's going to end
Because it's not always easy to fix and mend
It's easy to throw your life away.
Please make the most of it.

Pallvi Goutam (11)
Timbercroft Primary School, Plumstead

Beach Football Player

Fast runner
Ball kicker
Goal scorer
Good player
Opportunity tackler
Ball killer
Powerful jogger
Great glider
Slithering striker
Non cheater
Sports learner
Fast tackler
Penalty shooter
Fantastic scorer
Colour blaster
Blast passer
Swift slider
Ball bouncer
Cool curler.
What am I?

Shahir Ali (10)
Upton Cross Primary School, Plaistow

The Beach

I went to the beach,
I saw a massive leech.

Ah, no more!
But I'm full of bore.

The water shrieked,
Woah, it made me freak.

To see a liver,
It made me shiver.

Flying coconut,
I really need a hut.

The sun comes out,
I don't need to shout.

'Cause the children are giggling,
Why am I wriggling?
Maybe there are ants in my pants.

The gleaming sun
Is like a gigantic hot bun.

The colourful shells
Are rainbow bells.

When the crab
Makes me dab
At my poorly skin
Everything hurts, including my shin.

The flowery hats
Are not frightening bats.

The chips and fish
Are my daily dish.

Maisha Hussain (9)
Upton Cross Primary School, Plaistow

Midnight

When the sun goes down
And the stars come out,
There's a silent town,
Where the night-time creatures shout.

It's a scary place,
I'm running away, I hate it,
I'm on a fast pace,
So fast I'm getting fit.

I hid
In the shed,
I skid,
I hurt my head.

I'm so scared,
Even at work,
I really feared
While behind it lurked.

The night came,
There's no running away,
Went out did the fireplace flames,
I'm so wriggly, like blowing hay.

I can't go to bed,
I'm too terrified,
I slowly said,
'I'm too scared on the bad side.'

'Argh!' I screamed,
There's no need to do that,
I wished the sun beamed,
But then I saw bad creatures and a bat.

Nishat-Ara Ali (9)
Upton Cross Primary School, Plaistow

Sunny Beach

One day I walked through the lane,
Into a gigantic, heavy plane.

On my way to sunny Spain,
When I got there I had a game.

When I got to the beaches,
I ate a lot of peaches.

Grainy yellow sand,
Dropping through my hand.

Lots of people are insane,
Coming out of the massive plane.

So many dark blue waves,
Going into humongous caves.

I used my sun lotion
Before I went in the ocean.

I went to my friend's house,
I saw a giant big mouse.

I went back to the beach water,
It looked like it was going to slaughter.

I played my football match,
With my uncle, Mark Hatch.

I went to live in my hotel,
With my made-up fairy tale.

Yusuf Bobat (9)
Upton Cross Primary School, Plaistow

Beach

Grainy feeler
Happy maker
Rainy never
Light breezer
Sunny sighter
Lovely looker
Splash crasher
Guest seeker
Rapid riser
Magnificent viewer
Tremendous treasure
Peaceful pleasure
Sideways walker
Blue smasher
Precious granter
Kite flights.
What am I?

A: The beach.

Ayesha Kamran (10)
Upton Cross Primary School, Plaistow

The Beach

Breezy blower
Mercy maker
Sleek solid
Distance viewer
Super soggy
Great glider
Calmly relax
Fun playful
Boiling burning
Limp lighter
Fragile forever
Mushy moist
Swift speedy
Sparkly sporty
Who am I?

Thira Ul-Haq (9)
Upton Cross Primary School, Plaistow

My Sunny Holiday

I'm chillin' on the beach
Next to the sea that's deep.
Some girls and boys asked,
'Come 'n' play, it's just for today.'
I said, 'Pass it here,
Don't be a grumpy old dear.'
I'm sailing on sea that's so deep,
I see waves splashing on rocks,
Close to the slippery docks.
I see hats high and I ask,
'Where am I in the sky?'
The beach is so hot, hot, hot,
I'd better leave before I get polka dots.
Now it's time to go at the end of the day,
Back to sunny Spain.
I get on the aeroplane
And I get off the jumbo plane,
But I still feel pain.

Adham Chaudhary (10)
Upton Cross Primary School, Plaistow

Footballer

Goal scorer,
Great dribbler,
Award receiver,
Fair player,
Cup winner,
Opportunity taker,
Smart marker,
Free kicker,
Powerful shooter,
Crowd lover,
Rough tackler,
Cool curler,
Game starter,
Brisk slider,
Soccer saver.

Hassan Hussain (10)
Upton Cross Primary School, Plaistow

Football

Buzzing shoes
Goal scorer
Team saver
Hasty player
Excellent player
Extreme dribbler
Cool curler
Smart maker
Goal killer
Breath taker
Penalty taker
Love player
Cunning agile
Cup winner
Beach champion
Glory hunter
Match man
What am I?

Bilal Qureshi (10)
Upton Cross Primary School, Plaistow

Olympic Stadium

Beginning ceremony
Massive stadium
Busy streets
Crazy traffic
Children screaming
Encouraging adults
People eating
Uniting nations
Night light
Exciting events
Glory hunter
Marvellous medals
Terrific trophies
What am I?

Taneem Kirbria (9)
Upton Cross Primary School, Plaistow

On The Beach

I was relaxing on the beach one day
When I came across some children who wanted me to play.
We started playing tag when suddenly I tripped and hurt my back,
So I'd better go home and start to pack.

    I'm playin' with my friends!
    I'm playin' with my friends!

When I was on the beach, I lay down on the sand,
My parents bought me ice cream that I licked on the ground.

    I'm eating on the beach!
    I'm eating on the beach!

Maryam Ahmed (9)
Upton Cross Primary School, Plaistow

Jamming On The Beach

When I was walking on the beach one day,
A kite race was in my way.
I said to the kids, 'Your race is in my space!'
But oh, a boy complained to me,
'Your stinky breath is in my face.'
I was jamming on the beach one day
And I saw a zombie eat my friend, Claire.
I was thinking, *what just happened there?*

Abdullah Patel (9)
Upton Cross Primary School, Plaistow

Sunny Beach

I'm cruising on the beach, I'm cruising on the beach
I was on the beach one day
When I saw a kid and said, 'Hey!'
With my flip-flops I went to the little kid
And I did say, 'You shouldn't play without your mummy
Or you might hurt your tummy!'
I had some greasy hot dogs,
Then I went to the smelly bogs!

Razaool Haque (9)
Upton Cross Primary School, Plaistow

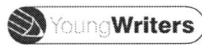

Anger

Anger is a raging bull
Ready to attack.

Anger is like a burning flame.

Anger feels as if there is
A rumbling earthquake in my brain.

Anger is a person locked away behind steel bars
Trying to get out.

Hannah Rockett (11)
Wormholt Park Primary School, Shepherd's Bush

Loneliness

Loneliness is grey, like a ghost wandering in the gloomy darkness.
It feels like being the only person left on the planet.
It feels like you are trying to get something, but can't feel it.
It smells like a fragrance that slowly fades away.
Loneliness is like a child sitting in a corner crying, but no one can hear them.

Abdirizak Ali (10)
Wormholt Park Primary School, Shepherd's Bush

Snowy Poem

Like a bolt from the blue it hits you
Sharp like an icicle
Like a sheep's white wool
Magical and rough
The taste from the frosty air
Very icy
As white as paper
Very clean like baby powder
The snow from a mountain
Like an ice cube
A creak from a tree
Like an owl whistling
The lumpy, big snow
Makes you feel heavy.

Patrick Ukagba (9)
Wyborne Primary School, New Eltham

Witch's Brew

Into the cauldron we must throw
A broken toe from a baby crow.
A grey whisker from an old, lumpy cat,
The smallest hair from a scabby rat.
An old, fat dragon's red and green scale,
A young man's skin nice and pale.
A fat little baby's first ever tear,
The left ear of a red and spotted deer.
Double, double, toil and trouble,
Fire burn and cauldron bubble.
The very tip of a white unicorn's horn,
The first hair from a newly born.
The thick blood from a wolf long dead,
The sticky slime from a slug's head.
A baby baboon's red little butt,
The blood from a baby giraffe's first ever cut.
A stinky chicken's largest brown feather,
A lock of hair from a girl named Heather.
A red boxing kangaroo's tiniest toenail,
Half a metre of red and blue sail.
A big, slow koala's shiniest hair,
A bit of rock from a dragon's lair.
Cool it with a human's ear
And you will have a potion of fear.

Owen Phelps (9)
Wyborne Primary School, New Eltham

Ice Palace Poem

The whisper of a little bird singing
Relaxed, relaxed, relaxed.
The whistle of the wonderful wind
Cold, cold, cold.
Crystal-white snow on the trees
Bright, bright, bright.
Bright blue, clear sky
Energetic, energetic, energetic.
A tatty wooden house sitting in the snow
Cheerful, cheerful, cheerful.

Conor Shiels (9)
Wyborne Primary School, New Eltham

Witches' Brew

'Double, double, toil and trouble
Fire burn and cauldron bubble'
Put into the charmed pot:
Some six-day-old human snot
A badger killed by two big rocks
And a baby with chickenpox
An ancient pear, old and dry
And a lizard that has only one eye
Two spiders that have only six legs
And a tramp who has to beg
One toad that hasn't got an ear
To make a potion which creates fear
'Double, double, toil and trouble
Fire burn and cauldron bubble'
A severed head chopped at noon
A werewolf who died on the moon
Burned skin from a toad
A hairy horse killed on a road
Two toes from a lord
The fresh blood from a sword
Mix it together with an arm from Macbeth
To make a potion that creates death.

William Guest (8)
Wyborne Primary School, New Eltham

Witches' Brew

Into the cauldron we must throw,
A beak of a nearly dead crow,
A whisker of a scabby cat,
A wing of a little bat,
A slimy eye from a tiny frog,
The disgusting mould from a giant log,
A tail of a lion fat,
The guts of an old ginger cat,
The remains of three mouldy nuts,
And some stripy tiger guts.

'Double, double, toil and trouble
Fire burn and cauldron bubble'.

Thomas Miller (8)
Wyborne Primary School, New Eltham

Witch's Spell

Round and round the bubbling pot,
Put all the things on the fiery spot.
Rubbery pig's nose and kangaroo intestines
All mouldy and small,
Round and round the bubbling pot,
Put all the things on the fiery spot.
Throw in squidgy dog snot,
Even worse fluffy horses' ears.
Round and round the bubbling pot,
Put all the things on the fiery spot.
Crinkly dog bones, crunch, crunch, crunch
And yucky orange ear wax.
Round and round the bubbling pot,
Put all the things on the fiery spot.
Throw in all the wriggly donkey tails
And the rotten granny teeth.
Round and round the bubbling pot,
Put all the things on the fiery spot.
Next, big fat stink bomb and damp flesh,
Round and round the bubbling pot,
Put all the things on the fiery spot.

Molly-Rose Heselden (8)
Wyborne Primary School, New Eltham

Snowy Poem

Quick as a bolt of lightning, the snow hits you
Cold as an icicle
It's too snowy, you can't see
You smell evil in the air
There's a cottage in the distance
You feel scared
The door is wide open
You move cautiously
The cottage looks empty and damp
You feel spooky, you don't go in
There are mountains in the distance
Suddenly you feel abandoned
The white snow crackles like Coco Pops.

Ella Hale (9)
Wyborne Primary School, New Eltham

Snowy Poem

The cold, wintry air,
Blowing in my face,
The everlasting coldness,
I can't bear it, not now,
I'm dreaming of a nice warm bed,
It will never come, that's for sure.
Whoever thought this cold, white stuff
Could be such a killing machine.
The children back at home,
They liked this stuff, it was not to be feared,
But out here there is a lot to be afraid of.
Mashed up rat, that's all I eat,
Boiled or stewed, fried or raw,
I long for a proper meal, anything but rat,
When it turns dark I can only hear bats.
Inside this shelter I lie all cold,
Cold and frightened, cold and awake,
I never get a decent night's sleep, I lay awake
Thinking and thinking of the things I've done wrong,
Can you guess where I am?
I'm lost, lost in the snow.

Benjamin Luxford (8)
Wyborne Primary School, New Eltham

I Am . . .

I am the beautiful, swooping, gliding owl
Who saved you from the deep, glittering snow.

I am the majestic, crystal-white polar bear
Who made the wolves scatter and go.

I am the whistling wind
Who will blow mighty obstacles in the way.

I am a speedy sleigh
To guide you on your fearsome journey, wherever you may travel.

I am a flaming, crackling, spitting fire
To give you warmth.

Luke Hazelton (9)
Wyborne Primary School, New Eltham

Witches' Brew

Into the cauldron we must throw
A long-footed crow
White, soft wool of a tiny little bat
The whisker of a scabby, blind cat
A rough, small leg of a nasty cruel lizard
A toe of a blind old wizard
The large, scary eye of a tremendous dinosaur
An ancient, manky tyrannosaur
The slimy, disgusting tongue of a skinny dog
And a frog from a missing bog.

'Double, double, toil and trouble
Fire burn and cauldron bubble'

The fat tooth of a silly girl
A rhino that had done a twirl
The clever human's intelligent brain
An old wheel of a rusty train
The cute chicken's sweet voice
Which of these would be your choice?
A thistle from a rose, in go all of those
Now the cauldron will bubble and make lots of trouble.

Subeeksha Jeyasangar (8)
Wyborne Primary School, New Eltham

Ice Palace Poem

A snowy winter wonderland
Excited, excited, excited.
Icy winds flying back and forth
As the day begins to set
Dreamy, dreamy, dreamy.
Dazzling stars shining on the soft snow
Magical, magical, magical.
Glittering icicles hanging in the moonlight
Sparkling, sparkling, sparkling.
Everywhere I look I see crystal-white snow
Beautiful, beautiful, beautiful.

Taylor Hollman (8)
Wyborne Primary School, New Eltham

Witches' Brew

'Double, double, toil and trouble
Fire burn and cauldron bubble'
Put into the charmed potion pot
Lava from a volcano bubbling hot
Whiskers from a scabby cat
Feathers from an ugly rat
Fingers from a witch's mummy
Boiled in a toad's tummy
A male bear's right, hairy ear
A little of a baby's tear
'Double, double, toil and trouble
Fire burn and cauldron bubble'
Into the cauldron we must throw
A little lion's skinny toe
Boiled in with camel's fat
Two mouldy toes of a vampire bat
Add 100 little newts
Then squeeze the mud off a Wellington boot
Cool it with a puppy's ear
And you will get a potion of fear.

Tunmishe Moronwiyan (8)
Wyborne Primary School, New Eltham

Ice Palace Poem

A snowy winter wonderland,
Excited, excited, excited.
Icy winds flying back and forth
As the day begins to set.
Dreamy, dreamy, dreamy.
Dazzling stars shining on the soft snow.
Magical, magical, magical.
Glittering icicles hanging in the moonlight.
Sparkling, sparkling, sparkling.
Everywhere I look I see crystal-white snow.
Beautiful, beautiful, beautiful.

Vinnie French-Gibbens (8)
Wyborne Primary School, New Eltham

Witches' Brew

Into the cauldron we must throw
Ten feathers of a mouldy crow,
A bucket full of shaking fear,
Along with a bear's juicy ear,
Chocolate made from old fat rat,
A lock of fur from a shrieking cat.
*'Double, double, toil and trouble
Fire burn and cauldron bubble'.*
Into the cauldron we must throw
A small brown snail that's very slow,
Fat children's juicy, well-preserved thighs,
With dear Henry's giant eyes.
The ear of a wolf baked and broke,
The tongue from a toad that's never had a croak.
Mix your potion round and round,
You might hear a popping sound.
Wait until it's nice and firm,
It will make your tummy churn.

Ella'mai Aldridge (8)
Wyborne Primary School, New Eltham

A Brand New Day

When I wake up and get out of my bed,
I look in the mirror and scratch my head.
I get to the bathroom but I'm usually last,
So I go downstairs and have some breakfast.
I pick out my favourite cereal but my brother's had most,
So I settle for two slices of toast.
I went to the toilet but it was blocked
And then my head sort of clocked.
Quick, get a hanger out of the cupboard,
Here comes nutty Mrs Hubbard.
I'm ready for school and leave the door,
It's cold outside with frost on the floor.
I'm late for school and start to run,
But then I fall over on my bum!
At school it's reading time, so I get a book,
But on my head was a big fat cook!

Sophie Luckett (8)
Wyborne Primary School, New Eltham

Dolphin Poem

Dolphins, dolphins all around
Their silver bellies flying around

There were dolphins all around
Their leaps were like an ark
Then we saw a shark

They were up in the air
To see who can jump the highest

They showered Zoey with dolphin drops
From the sea and up above

They rocked the boat
They showered us
But that's not all, they could move us

Zoey glided her hands
Through the see-through water

Then she stopped!

Chloe French (9)
Wyborne Primary School, New Eltham

Snowy Poem

So pale and white,
You jump up with fright.
You can whisper a song,
But not for long.
Like a bolt out of the blue,
The snow hits you.
You cry in pain,
As you walk along the lane.
You smell evil in the air,
And think foul is fair.
Just as you sit on an icy chair,
Oh, the mountains so very high,
Snow falling down from the sky.
Trees covered in a sheet of snow,
And the temperature oh so very low.
Everything in winter is always slow.

Anumita Mukherjee (9)
Wyborne Primary School, New Eltham

Snowy Poem

Piles of snow on the trees, too many to count
I feel small, lonely and cold
The sky is frosty
The floor is white and fluffy
It feels amazing
It tastes like frozen air
I feel isolated but good
When I walk the snow creaks
I feel like I'm being pulled down
As the snow is so heavy on my boots
I am so cold
I feel like an ice cube melting
My gloves are wet
I've been throwing snowballs at trees
Icicles falling from up high, drip, drop, drip
As the day ends I fall asleep in my warm and cosy bed
And I remember that day in the snow.

Sydney Cammiss-Brown (9)
Wyborne Primary School, New Eltham

Letter To Walter

Dear Walter,
Please come back to the farm,
Without you my life isn't calm.
Come back to Devon, it's better than Heaven.
I'm always in my bed, all these memories in my head.
So as you can see, please come back to me!
I put that thing into my nan's tea,
It worked, now I'm not mad.
I know it's bad what I said to you.
When you're gone, a part of me is missing.
I hope you are listening to this letter,
It will be better if you're back.
All that anger that I let out has gone,
Where I don't know.
If you come back I'll only be good,
I would never be mad with you.

Louie Cameron (8)
Wyborne Primary School, New Eltham

Witch's Spell

Fiery broth and witch's brew,
Snails' shells and lizards too.
Fiery broth and witch's brew,
Fly into the witch's magic,
You will feel absolutely tragic.
Fiery broth and witch's brew,
When you add a fly it will die.
Fiery broth and witch's brew,
Add a goblin head instead
And you'll be dead.
Fiery broth and witch's brew
To make it taste like a nettle and a kettle
And for that extra taste add some frog paste.
Fiery broth and witch's brew,
Add some maggots too!

Lydia Hackwood (8)
Wyborne Primary School, New Eltham

Remembrance Poem

R emember those brave soldiers
E ven though they are dead
M ightily they went out to fight for our rights
E verlasting peace is what they wished for
M aybe others loved to fight
B loodshed and gore the wars led to
R unning around our brave boys
A s they fought
N ot knowing if they would live
C ircles we make to remember them
E vil will just never die.

Oliver Hayhoe (9)
Wyborne Primary School, New Eltham

Ice Palace Poem

A snowy winter wonderland,
Excited, excited, excited.
Icy winds flying back and forth
As the day begins to set,
Dreamy, dreamy, dreamy.
Dazzling stars shining on the soft snow,
Magical, magical, magical.
Glittering icicles hanging in the moonlight,
Sparkling, sparkling, sparkling.
Everywhere I look I see crystal-white snow,
Beautiful, beautiful, beautiful.

Luke Redburn (9)
Wyborne Primary School, New Eltham

Ice Palace Poem

Wind hustling around you,
Hustle, hustle, hustle.
Feeling like an ice cube,
Cube, cube, cube.
Icicles dropping at night,
Drop, drop, drop.
Tall, snow-covered trees swaying gently to the east,
East, east, east.
Snow spitting from the air,
Snow, snow, snow.

Eric Bui (9)
Wyborne Primary School, New Eltham

Ice Palace Poem

Snow spitting from the air,
Stunned, stunned, stunned.

Clear blue sky,
Relax, relax, relax.

Ice cubes as hard as a rock,
To crack a chestnut.

Saleh Ali (9)
Wyborne Primary School, New Eltham

Ice Palace Poem

Snow spitting from the air,
Dreamy, dreamy, dreamy.
Crystal-white treetops,
Stunned, stunned, stunned.
Dazzling trees with glittering snow
Falling on top of them.
Magical, magical, magical.
Trees covered with snow,
Kids playing, parents watching.

Kirat Singh Chana (9)
Wyborne Primary School, New Eltham

I Am . . .

I am the beautiful, swooping, gliding owl
Who saved you from the deep, glittering snow.
I am the majestic, crystal-white polar bear
Who made the wolves scatter and go.
I am the whistling wind
Who will blow mighty obstacles in the way.
I am a speedy sleigh to guide you on your fearsome journey
Wherever you may travel.
I am a flaming, crackling, steaming fire to give you warmth.

Diante Grant (8)
Wyborne Primary School, New Eltham

Ice Palace

Snow spitting from the blue, shiny sky,
Amazed, amazed, amazed.
Crystal-white snow on the treetops,
Cold, cold, cold.
A tattered wooden house is cold and frosty,
Dreamy, dreamy, dreamy.
Echoes in the dark, gloomy forest,
Scared, scared, scared.

Sam Bennett (8)
Wyborne Primary School, New Eltham

Poppy Prediction

Remember, remember the 11th of November,
When soldiers risked their lives for the United Kingdom.
Kids from school who join the army to save us,
Suffering from the gunfire.
Every year we have a remembrance assembly
To remember the people who died in the war.

Kelly Delohery (9)
Wyborne Primary School, New Eltham

Fear

Fear is red, like a burning flame.
It tastes salty like the River Thames.
It smells like nothing, everything is smudged like a cloudy winter's day.
My ears pop like I'm on a plane.
My tummy bubbles like a cooking pot.
That's fear.

Sachin Thorogood (8)
Wyborne Primary School, New Eltham

I Am . . .

I am the quiet owl flying in the night sky.
I am the frozen icicle glittering like a diamond.
I am the blustering snow blowing through the night.
I am the wrinkly old woman collecting your tears.
I am the bear who scared off the wolves.
I am the spruce tree that saved you from the avalanche.

Elise Hodson (9)
Wyborne Primary School, New Eltham

Remembrance Poem

Poppies for peace
We remember how you saved us
We remember how you won the battle
You are our heroes
We will remember you always.

Tommy Delohery (9)
Wyborne Primary School, New Eltham

I Am . . .

I am the icicle that hung down and shone in the sun.
I am the grizzly bear that shook its fur as fast as the wind.
I am the furry tree that you can cuddle in the cold, brisk air.
I am the sparkling snow which moves like a whisper.
I am the old lady with my glittery coat and my sly words.
I am the owl that is as white as snow that has just fallen.

Leila McQuillen (9)
Wyborne Primary School, New Eltham

I Am . . .

I am the feathery owl who led you back to shelter
I am also the grizzly bear who scared the scary wolves away
I am the wrinkly old woman that you cannot be
I am the tall fir tree that saved you from the rocks
I am the glittery icicle that was twinkling in the sunlight
I am the snowy snowdrift that gave you a miracle.

Max Morton (8)
Wyborne Primary School, New Eltham

I Am . . .

I am the white owl that leads you back to your safe den.
I am the brown bear that scared all the wolves away.
I am the icicle that's as glittery as a diamond.
I am the spruce tree that saved you from the rushing avalanche.
I am the snow that helped you build your snow den.
I am not the old lady you think I am.

Luke Ogunbameru (8)
Wyborne Primary School, New Eltham

Ballerina Poem

Her beautiful eyes sparkled like the stars
Her hair curls like a glitter shell
Her dazzling dress takes people's breath away
Her dancing will leave a tear in your eye
The way she tiptoes is remarkable.

Jaiden Ismond (8)
Wyborne Primary School, New Eltham

Fear

Fear is red like fire
It tastes like chilli con carne
It smells like mouldy oranges
It looks like you're in front of a crowd
It sounds like people screaming
It feels like burning hot lava.

Mia Bennett (9)
Wyborne Primary School, New Eltham

Snowy Poem

As blank as a sheet of paper.
It feels like you're melting in the snow.
The beautiful scene that tastes like the frosty, cold air.
It looks like baby powder.
It's like millions of sprinkles with sugar.
Sparkling icicles twinkling in the snow.

Sandra Jacek (9)
Wyborne Primary School, New Eltham

Strong Man

His muscles are as strong as a rock
And he is a generous man.
He has a big moustache,
Sharp as a shark's tooth.
Also he has a skeleton tattoo on his arm.

Muhammed Ali Gunebakan (8)
Wyborne Primary School, New Eltham

Maddie's Workshop

FEATURED AUTHOR:

Maddie Stewart

Maddie is a children's writer, poet and author who currently lives in Coney Island, Northern Ireland.

Maddie has 5 published children's books, 'Cinders', 'Hal's Sleepover', 'Bertie Rooster', 'Peg' and 'Clever Daddy'. Maddie uses her own unpublished work to provide entertaining, interactive poems and rhyming stories for use in her workshops with children when she visits schools, libraries, arts centres and book festivals. Favourites are 'Silly Billy, Auntie Millie' and 'I'm a Cool, Cool Kid'. Maddie works throughout Ireland from her home in County Down. She is also happy to work from a variety of bases in England. She has friends and family, with whom she regularly stays, in Leicester, Bedford, London and Ashford (Kent). Maddie's workshops are aimed at 5-11-year-olds. Check out Maddie's website for all her latest news and free poetry resources **www.maddiestewart.com**.

Read on to pick up some fab writing tips!

Nonsense Workshop

If you find silliness fun, you will love nonsense poems. Nonsense poems might describe silly things, or people, or situations, or, any combination of the three.

For example:

When I got out of bed today,
both my arms had run away.
I sent my feet to fetch them back.
When they came back, toe in hand
I realised what they had planned.
They'd made the breakfast I love most,
buttered spider's eggs on toast.

One way to find out if you enjoy nonsense poems is to start with familiar nursery rhymes. Ask your teacher to read them out, putting in the names of some children in your class.

Like this: Troy and Jill went up the hill
to fetch a pail of water.
Troy fell down
and broke his crown
and Jill came tumbling after.

If anyone is upset at the idea of using their name, then don't use it.

Did you find this fun?

Maddie's Workshop

**Now try changing a nursery rhyme.
Keep the rhythm and the rhyme style, but invent a silly situation.**

Like this: Hickory Dickory Dare
a pig flew up in the air.
The clouds above
gave him a shove
Hickory Dickory Dare.

Or this: Little Miss Mabel
sat at her table
eating a strawberry pie
but a big, hairy beast
stole her strawberry feast
and made poor little Mabel cry.

How does your rhyme sound if you put your own name in it?

Another idea for nonsense poems is to pretend letters are people and have them do silly things.

For example:
Mrs A   Mrs B   Mrs C
Lost her way   Dropped a pea   Ate a tree

**To make your own 'Silly People Poem', think of a word to use.
To show you an example, I will choose the word 'silly'.
Write your word vertically down the left hand side of your page.
Then write down some words which rhyme
with the sound of each letter.**

S mess, dress, Bess, chess, cress
I eye, bye, sky, guy, pie, sky
L sell, bell, shell, tell, swell, well
L " " " " " (" means the same as written above)
Y (the same words as those rhyming with I)

Use your rhyming word lists to help you make up your poem.

Mrs S made a mess
Mrs I ate a pie
Mrs L rang a bell
Mrs L broke a shell
Mrs Y said 'Bye-bye.'

You might even make a 'Silly Alphabet' by using all the letters of the alphabet.

It is hard to find rhyming words for all the letters. H, X and W are letters which are hard to match with rhyming words. I'll give you some I've thought of:

H - cage, stage, wage (close but not perfect)
X - flex, specs, complex, Middlesex
W - trouble you, chicken coop, bubble zoo

However, with nonsense poems, you can use nonsense words. You can make up your own words.

To start making up nonsense words you could try mixing dictionary words together. Let's make up some nonsense animals.

Make two lists of animals. (You can include birds and fish as well.)

Your lists can be as long as you like. These are lists I made:

elephant	kangaroo
tiger	penguin
lizard	octopus
monkey	chicken

Now use the start of an animal on one list and substitute it for the start of an animal from your other list.

I might use the start of oct/opus ... oct and substitute it for the end of l/izard to give me a new nonsense animal ... an octizard.
I might swap the start of monk/ey ... monk with the end of kang/aroo
To give me another new nonsense animal ... a monkaroo.

What might a monkaroo look like? What might it eat?

You could try mixing some food words in the same way, to make up nonsense foods.

cabbage	potatoes
lettuce	parsley
bacon	crisps

Cribbage, bacley, and lettatoes are some nonsense foods made up from my lists.

Let's see if I can make a nonsense poem about my monkaroo.

Maddie's Workshop

My monkaroo loves bacley.
He'll eat lettatoes too
But his favourite food is cribbage
Especially if it's blue.

Would you like to try and make up your own nonsense poem?

**Nonsense words don't have to be a combination of dictionary words.
They can be completely 'made up'.
You can use nonsense words to write nonsense sonnets,
or list poems or any type of poem you like.**

Here is a poem full of nonsense words:

I melly micked a turdle
and flecked a pendril's tum.
I plotineyed a shugat
and dracked a pipin's plum.

Ask your teacher to read it putting in some children's names instead of the first I, and he or she instead of the second I.

Did that sound funny?

You might think that nonsense poems are just silly and not for the serious poet. However poets tend to love language. Making up your own words is a natural part of enjoying words and sounds and how they fit together. Many poets love the freedom nonsense poems give them. Lots and lots of very famous poets have written nonsense poems. I'll name some: **Edward Lear, Roger McGough, Lewis Carroll, Jack Prelutsky** and **Nick Toczek**. Can you or your teacher think of any more? For help with a class nonsense poem or to find more nonsense nursery rhymes look on my website, **www.maddiestewart.com**. Have fun! Maddie Stewart.

Poetry Techniques

Here is a selection of poetry techniques with examples

Metaphors & Similes

A *metaphor* is when you describe your subject *as* something else, for example: 'Winter is a cruel master leaving the servants in a bleak wilderness' whereas a *simile* describes your subject *like* something else i.e. 'His blue eyes are like ice-cold puddles' or 'The flames flickered like eyelashes'.

Personification

This is to simply give a personality to something that is not human, for example 'Fear spreads her uneasiness around' or 'Summer casts down her warm sunrays'.

Imagery

To use words to create mental pictures of what you are trying to convey, your poem should awaken the senses and make the reader feel like they are in that poetic scene ...
'The sky was streaked with pink and red as shadows cast across the once-golden sand'.
'The sea gently lapped the shore as the palm trees rustled softly in the evening breeze'.

Assonance & Alliteration

Alliteration uses a repeated constant sound and this effect can be quite striking: 'Smash, slippery snake slithered sideways'.
Assonance repeats a significant vowel or vowel sound to create an impact: 'The pool looked cool'.

Poetry Techniques

Repetition

By repeating a significant word the echo effect can be a very powerful way of enhancing an emotion or point your poem is putting across.
'The blows rained down, down,
Never ceasing,
Never caring
About the pain,
The pain'.

Onomatopoeia

This simply means you use words that sound like the noise you are describing, for example 'The rain *pattered* on the window' or 'The tin can *clattered* up the alley'.

Rhythm & Metre

The *rhythm* of a poem means 'the beat', the sense of movement you create. The placing of punctuation and the use of syllables affect the *rhythm* of the poem. If your intention is to have your poem read slowly, use double, triple or larger syllables and punctuate more often, where as if you want to have a fast-paced read use single syllables, less punctuation and shorter sentences.
If you have a regular rhythm throughout your poem this is known as *metre*.

Enjambment

This means you don't use punctuation at the end of your line, you simply let the line flow on to the next one. It is commonly used and is a good word to drop into your homework!

Tone & Lyric

The poet's intention is expressed through their *tone*. You may feel happiness, anger, confusion, loathing or admiration for your poetic subject. Are you criticising or praising? How you feel about your topic will affect your choice of words and therefore your *tone*. For example 'I *loved* her', 'I *cared* for her', 'I *liked* her'.
If you write the poem from a personal view or experience this is referred to as a *lyrical* poem. A good example of a lyrical poem is Seamus Heaney's 'Mid-term Break' or any sonnet!

All About Shakespeare

Try this fun quiz with your family, friends or even in class!

1. Where was Shakespeare born?

....

2. Mercutio is a character in which Shakepeare play?

....

3. Which monarch was said to be 'quite a fan' of his work?

....

4. How old was he when he married?

....

5. What is the name of the last and 'only original' play he wrote?

....

6. What are the names of King Lear's three daughters?

....

7. Who is Anne Hathaway?

....

All About Shakespeare

8. Which city is the play 'Othello' set in?

....

9. Can you name 2 of Shakespeare's 17 comedies?

....

10. 'This day is call'd the feast of Crispian: He that outlives this day, and comes safe home, Will stand a tip-toe when this day is nam'd, and rouse him at the name of Crispian' is a quote from which play?

....

11. Leonardo DiCaprio played Romeo in the modern day film version of Romeo and Juliet. Who played Juliet in the movie?

....

12. Three witches famously appear in which play?

....

13. Which famous Shakespearean character is Eric in the image to the left?

....

14. What was Shakespeare's favourite poetic form?

....

Answers are printed on the last page of the book, good luck!

If you would rather try the quiz online,
you can do so at www.youngwriters.co.uk.

POETRY ACTIVITY

Word Soup

To help you write a poem, or even a story, on any theme, you should create word soup!

If you have a theme or subject for your poem, base your word soup on it. If not, don't worry, the word soup will help you find a theme.

To start your word soup you need ingredients:

- Nouns (names of people, places, objects, feelings, i.e. Mum, Paris, house, anger)
- Colours
- Verbs ('doing words', i.e. kicking, laughing, running, falling, smiling)
- Adjectives (words that describe nouns, i.e. tall, hairy, hollow, smelly, angelic)

We suggest at least 5 of each from the above list, this will make sure your word soup has plenty of choice. Now, if you have already been given a theme or title for your poem, base your ingredients on this. If you have no idea what to write about, write down whatever you like, or ask a teacher or family member to give you a theme to write about.

Poetry Activity

Making Word Soup

Next, you'll need a sheet of paper.
Cut it into at least 20 pieces. Make sure the pieces are big enough to write your ingredients on, one ingredient on each piece of paper.
Write your ingredients on the pieces of paper.
Shuffle the pieces of paper and put them all in a box or bowl - something you can pick the paper out of without looking at the words.
Pick out 5 words to start and use them to write your poem!

Example:

Our theme is winter. Our ingredients are:
- Nouns: snowflake, Santa, hat, Christmas, snowman.
- Colours: blue, white, green, orange, red.
- Verbs: ice-skating, playing, laughing, smiling, wrapping.
- Adjectives: cold, tall, fast, crunchy, sparkly.

**Our word soup gave us these 5 words:
snowman, red, cold, hat, fast and our poem goes like this:**

It's a *cold* winter's day,
My nose and cheeks are *red*
As I'm outside, building my *snowman*,
I add a *hat* and a carrot nose to finish,
I hope he doesn't melt too *fast*!

Tip: add more ingredients to your word soup and see how many different poems you can write!

Tip: if you're finding it hard to write a poem with the words you've picked, swap a word with another one!

Tip: try adding poem styles and techniques, such as assonance or haiku to your soup for an added challenge!

SCRIBBLER!

*If you enjoy creative writing then you'll love our magazine, Scribbler!, the fun and educational magazine for 7-11-year-olds that works alongside Key Stage 2 National Literacy Strategy Learning Objectives. For further information visit **www.youngwriters.co.uk**.*

Grammar Fun
Our resident dinosaur Bernard helps to improve writing skills from punctuation to spelling.

Nessie's Workshop
Each issue Nessie explains a style of writing and sets an exercise for you to do. Previous workshops include the limerick, haiku and shape poems.

Awesome Author
Read all about past and present authors. Previous Awesome Authors include Roald Dahl, William Shakespeare and Ricky Gervais!

Once Upon a Time ...
Lord Oscar starts a story ... it's your job to finish it. Our favourite wins a writing set.

Guest Author
A famous author drops by and answers some of our in-depth questions, while donating a great prize to give away. Recent authors include former Children's Laureate Michael Morpurgo, adventurer Bear Grylls and Nick Ward, author of the Charlie Small Journals.

Art Gallery
Send Bizzy your paintings and drawings and his favourite wins an art set including some fab Staedtler goodies.

Puzzle Time!
Could you find Eric? Unscramble Anna Gram's words? Tackle our hard puzzles? If so, winners receive fab prizes.

Homework Help With Bronte
Scribbler!'s own Bronte is always on hand to help with spellings, alternative words and writing styles, she'll get you on the right track!

Prizes
Every issue we give away fantastic prizes. Recent prizes include Staedtler goodies, signed copies of Bear Grylls' books and posters, signed copies of Ricky Gervais' books, Charlie Small goodie bags, family tickets to The Eden Project, The Roald Dahl Museum & Story Centre and Alton Towers, a digital camera, books and writing sets galore and many other fab prizes!

... plus much more!
We keep you up to date with all the happenings in the world of literature, including recent updates from the current Children's Laureate.

*If you are too old for Scribbler! magazine or have an older friend who enjoys creative writing, then check out Wordsmith. Wordsmith is for 11-18-year-olds and is jam-packed full of brilliant features, young writers' work, competitions and interviews too. For further information check out **www.youngwriters.co.uk** or ask an adult to call us on (01733) 890066.*

To get an adult to subscribe to either magazine for you, ask them to visit the website or give us a call.

Once Upon a Rhyme 2011 - London

Young Writers Information

We hope you have enjoyed reading this book - and that you will continue to enjoy it in the coming years.

If you like reading and writing poetry drop us a line, or give us a call, and we'll send you a free information pack.

Alternatively, if you would like to order further copies of this book or any of our other titles, then please give us a call or log onto our website at www.youngwriters.co.uk.

Young Writers Information
Remus House
Coltsfoot Drive
Peterborough
PE2 9BF
Tel: (01733) 890066
Fax: (01733) 313524

Email: info@youngwriters.co.uk

Shakespeare Quiz Answers

1. Stratford-upon-Avon **2.** Romeo and Juliet **3.** James I **4.** 18 **5.** The Tempest **6.** Regan, Cordelia and Goneril **7.** His wife **8.** Venice **9.** All's Well That Ends Well, As You Like It, The Comedy of Errors, Cymbeline, Love's Labour's Lost, Measure for Measure, The Merchant of Venice, The Merry Wives of Windsor, A Midsummer Night's Dream, Much Ado About Nothing, Pericles - Prince of Tyre, The Taming of the Shrew, The Tempest, Twelfth Night, The Two Gentlemen of Verona, Troilus & Cressida, The Winter's Tale **10.** Henry V **11.** Claire Danes **12.** Macbeth **13.** Hamlet **14.** Sonnet